Luther's Meditations on the Gospels

Luther's Meditations on the Gospels

Translated and Arranged by
Roland H. Bainton

Illustrated with Woodcuts by
Virgil Solis

James Clarke & Co.

James Clarke & Co.

P.O. Box 60
Cambridge
CB1 2NT
United Kingdom

www.jamesclarke.co
publishing@jamesclarke.co

Hardback ISBN: 978 0 227 17962 8
Paperback ISBN: 978 0 227 17954 3
PDF ISBN: 978 0 227 17953 6
ePub ISBN: 978 0 227 17955 0

British Library Cataloguing in Publication Data
A record is available from the British Library

First published by The Lutterworth Press, 1963
This edition published by James Clarke & Co., 2023

Copyright © W.L. Jenkins, 1963

All rights reserved. No part of this edition may be reproduced, stored electronically or in any retrieval system, or transmitted in any form or by any means, electronic, mechanical, photocopying, recording, or otherwise, without prior written permission from the Publisher (permissions@jamesclarke.co).

*To
Heinrich Bornkamm
who has so greatly enriched our
understanding of Luther*

Contents

Introduction		1
1	The Coming of the Redeemer	11
2	Beginnings of the Ministry	28
3	The Sermon on the Mount	41
4	The Miracles and the Parables	54
5	The Journey to Jerusalem and Holy Week	71
6	The Lord's Supper	89
7	Arrest and Trial	102
8	The Crucifixion	117
9	The Resurrection	127
Sources		141

Introduction

Can the bones of Luther's sermons live again? Not all of them certainly. There are too many. A modern German rendering of Luther's sermons on the Gospels makes five huge volumes of nearly three thousand pages. Besides, some of the bones are vestigial and of interest only to historical specialists. If Luther is to be widely read in our day, he will have to be excerpted. That which is selected must have an element of the universal, yet, if it is completely denuded of its temporal vestments, it will be only naked spirit. Great preaching is that which relates the timeless to time, and it cannot be transferred to another time simply by divesting it of all reference to its own era. For that reason, the effort has been made here to select from Luther's sermons passages that deal not only with man as man but also with man as German. No equivalents have been substituted for the names of coins—heller, florin, and gulden. References remain to the Reichstag, the Kaiser, and to such places as Wittenberg, Erfurt, and the Joachimstal. Thus Luther prompts us not to repeat his preaching but to imitate it by doing for our time what he did for his.

We should bear in mind, incidentally, that the problem of translating into the terms of another age applies not only to Luther but to the Gospels themselves. They were written years ago against a Palestinian background of simple, rural communities occupied with sowing, reaping, fishing, tanning, and carrying water from the well. Luther's setting was actually closer to that of the Gospels than is our own.

Take for example two sayings from the Sermon on the Mount—

"Ye are the light of the world" and "Ye are the salt of the earth." The first referring to light is universal if light be simply light. At this point there has been no change in a million years. But if we go on and read, "Which of you takes a lamp?" then we are in the age that preceded the incandescent bulb. Again, "Ye are the salt of the earth." Salt as a seasoning is universal, but salt as a preservative has been superseded by refrigeration. If one would convey the full sense of these sayings, whether in the Gospels or in Luther, one has to explain how salt formerly was used!

Luther is removed from us not only by the outward aspects of his culture but even more profoundly by a state of mind. He belonged to the Middle Ages in his envelopment by the supernatural. Heaven then lay close to earth. Angels, saints, and demons hovered over the abodes of men. To whom among us would it ever have occurred, as it did to Luther, that the Virgin Mary, when the boy Jesus was lost, should have reproached herself with the thought that because of her negligence God had taken his Son back to heaven and had decided not to save the world after all? Luther, indeed, protested against the childishness of regarding God's throne as if it were set up in a cardboard heaven. Yet, he had about him much of the spirit of his own little Hans and Magdalene whose simplicity he envied.

In other respects, however, he broke with the tradition of the Middle Ages and stands therefore nearer to us or rather we to him by reason of his break. He dropped the lush profusion of the legendary and adhered strictly to the text of the Gospels. The age of Gothic drew as heavily from the apocryphal as from the canonical gospels, in which, for example, we are told only that Wise Men came from the East. Nothing is said as to their number or rank. The early church began to make them into kings and to make their number three. Not till the tenth century did the artists give them crowns. The names Balthasar, Caspar, and Melchior cannot be traced back farther than the sixth century, and not until the fourteenth was one of them given the features of a Negro. By then the three had come to be regarded as representatives of the three races of mankind, the European, the Asiatic, and the African. Luther discarded all of these accretions for himself, though others might believe them if they liked. The legends of the Virgin Mary were similarly rejected, save for one little detail from the apocryphal gospels that Mary was fourteen years of age when confided to Joseph.

The allegory so dear to the Middle Ages, Luther almost entirely left behind. One could hardly expect him not to see in the Good Samaritan the figure of Christ, but in the case of turning water into wine he did not in medieval fashion equate the water with the Old Testament and the wine with the New, though he did have an allegory of his own in that the water stood for the tribulations and the wine for the joys of marriage.

The typology, which from the days of the early church linked the Old Testament and the New, was not repudiated as such by Luther. He too viewed history as a symphony of redemption in which certain themes recurred with variations from the creation of the world until their resolution in Christ. The suffering of Abel foreshadowed the suffering of Christ. The readiness of Isaac to be sacrificed was a foretaste of the sacrifice of Christ. But the stereotyped crudities of the illuminated manuscripts and the block books of the late Middle Ages disappeared in Luther. In those works a scene from the Gospels was flanked by two typological anticipations from the Old Testament. Christ going down into the tomb had on either side Joseph being let down into the well and Jonah being swallowed by the whale. The resurrection was flanked by Jonah emerging from the whale but not by Joseph being lifted out of the pit. Instead, there was Samson carrying off the gates of the city as Christ broke down the gates of hell. A whole series of such triptychs had become conventional. Luther instead treated the Old Testament stories with a graphic human realism and only in the profundities of human experience discovered the patterns of God's dealings with humankind.

The same treatment was applied to the New Testament. With what poignancy Luther imagined the distress of Mary when her son was lost! The quaint fancy that she thought God might have taken him back to heaven does not obscure for us all the anguish of uncertainty and all the self-recrimination with which she reproached herself. Then the joy that follows pain and the unfathomable paradox that God must first cast down before he can exalt! When Luther meditates on the love of God, on the utter self-emptying of Christ, on the inexpressible humility of the Lord of life, on the power of God's grace to strike a man dead and make him alive, to rout Satan, swallow death, and confer eternal life, how he makes one tremble for fright and quake for joy!

The following material has been taken entirely from Luther's sermons and lectures on the Gospels. In the selection of the excerpts an eye has been had to the piquant, the poignant, and the profound, and at the same time to the comprehensive, both as to the Gospels and as to Luther's ideas. Certainly all the essential themes of the Evangelists are here. If there is little of the eschatological, it is because Luther's interest did not center here, and there is no treatment of the transfiguration, the Gadarene swine, and the withered fig tree because on these themes Luther was not at his best. His own primary emphases are recurrent: the utter marvel of God's love; the salvation of man solely through divine grace and human faith; the futility of man's endeavor to gain a claim upon God and the sheer wonder of the forgiveness of sins; the insistence that though sins be forgiven, sin does not cease and yet that man should not acquiesce in his imperfection and cease to strive.

Much of Luther's preaching was polemical and here arises a doubt whether such portions should be repeated lest they revive the confessional animosities of the sixteenth century. But if they be left out, we shall miss the measure of the man. He lived in the midst of strife. For twenty-five years he was in imminent danger of the stake and was saved only because the emperor was too busy fighting the French, the Turk, and the pope to come to Germany and enforce the Edict of Worms against Luther. Therefore when he talked about the narrow gate, the little flock, the bearing of the cross, his words had a stark realism, intelligible fully only to those who in our day have felt in their flesh the calamities of this century.

The polemic refers not always to the Church of Rome but also to the radicals in Luther's own circle whose attack shook him even more because completely unexpected. Mention in the following sermons will be found to Carlstadt, whom Luther called a Spiritualist because he regarded the physical and sensory as inappropriate for the communication of the divine, which comes only through the

Introduction

Spirit. For that reason, Carlstadt rejected images and church music and denied any physical presence of Christ in the Lord's Supper. Luther's reply as to the latter point well appears in the excerpts. One rejoinder requires a comment. Luther found a confirmation of his view in that at the baptism of Jesus the presence of the Spirit did not suffice to proclaim the Lamb of God, but John had to point to him with his physical finger. Now the Gospel says nothing about the finger. Luther must have had in mind a picture like that of Grünewald in which John points with a highly elongated finger.

As for Luther on the Lord's Supper, since the subject was so controverted alike with the Catholics and the Spiritualists, Luther had occasion to deal with it frequently and with varying emphases. For that reason it has seemed best to set up the illustrative excerpts in a topical arrangement but to attach to each its date.

Mention also is made of the Anabaptists, who held that since baptism rests on faith and babies do not have faith, babies should not be baptized. Luther never managed that one very well. In our excerpt he has an amazing argument from the case of the unborn John the Baptist, who leaped in the womb when Mary greeted his mother, Elizabeth, thus showing his responsiveness to the Spirit even prior to birth.

Another figure mentioned is Thomas Müntzer, an inflammatory enthusiast, who summoned the elect to usher in the day of the Lord by the slaughter of the ungodly. Luther believed that the minister should never take the sword in defense of the gospel but only the magistrate in the keeping of the peace. The distinction of the two kingdoms, or administrations—the spiritual and the civil—is a constant theme.

The woodcuts accompanying the text are taken from an epitome of Luther's Bible published by his onetime amanuensis Veit Dietrich in 1562 at Frankfurt with the title *Summaria*. These cuts mark a departure in the history of gospel iconography. The artist signed himself "VS," standing for Virgil Solis. He was a resident of Nürnberg, born in 1514, who died in his forty-eighth year in 1562. His output was so vast that some have been tempted to try to advance the date of his death in order to get it all in. The German encyclopedia of artists (*Künstler Lexikon*) says that his best work consisted in his Biblical illustrations. These were his finest and his most German production. He is not to be compared with Dürer and Cranach, but he is by no means contemptible in craftsmanship and imagination.

The significance of the cuts appears to me to lie in the introduction of a new style of gospel iconography. The validation of this statement requires that one go back to the thirteenth century as a point of departure. With reference to this period, Emile Mâle has observed[1] that the themes in the life of Christ illustrated in the manuscripts and cathedrals were taken from the beginning and the end, from the Nativity and the Passion, whereas with rare exceptions there was no portrayal of the events and sayings of the public ministry. The reason, he surmised, was to be found in the liturgy. The two great festivals of the church year were Christmas and Easter. Christmas called for the graphic representation of the Annunciation, visitation, the birth, the presentation in the Temple, the flight into Egypt, and the massacre of the innocents. The Christmas cycle included Epiphany, on which was celebrated the arrival of the three kings on Twelfth-night, as well as the baptism of Jesus and the miracle at Cana. These last two went back to very primitive Christian beliefs and practices. In the early church the Adoptionists believed the baptism to have constituted the birth of the man Jesus as the Son of God when the Spirit entered into him at the baptism. When this belief was rejected, the continued celebration of the baptism as well as the birth on January 6 was justified on the assumption that Jesus was baptized exactly on his thirtieth birthday. The commemoration of the miracle at Cana had its origin in a Christian counter to the Epiphany of Dionysus who on January 6 turned water into wine. When this motive was forgotten the practice was again justified on the assumption that the miracle took place on the thirty-first birthday.

The Easter cycle might reach forward to include the ascension and even Pentecost and backward to embrace Lent, which called for the commemoration of the temptation for forty days and commonly also included the transfiguration.

---

1. Emile Mâle, *The Gothic Image* (Harper & Brothers, 1958, from the French of 1913), p. 178.

These, then, were the only events in the life of Christ to be illustrated. What Mâle has observed for the West in the thirteenth century, Millet has shown to be true also in the East for the fourteenth through the sixteenth centuries.[2] Dürer likewise was in the same tradition, for he covered the Nativity in his *Marienleben* and did two series of woodcuts on the Passion but nothing on the public ministry of Christ.

The pre-Lutheran—printed German Bibles, seventeen in number, exhibit a much greater parsimony of illustration. There were two types. The style for the first was set by the Pflanzmann Bible of 1470, which was followed by the two editions of Sorg in 1477 and 1480, the two by Zainer in 1473 and 1477, and by the edition of Sensenschmidt in 1472. In these Bibles there is a large woodcut of the Creation, but thereafter the only illustrations are the figures of men for the prophets, evangelists, and apostles. The life of Christ is not illustrated at all.

The second type was set by the Cologne Bible of 1480, to be followed by the Koburger in 1483, Strassburg 1485, Schönspurger 1487, Othmar 1507 and 1518, and Trutebul 1520. The modern reader, who has not access to the originals,[3] can study the types in the facsimile edition of the Strassburg Bible in the edition of Paul Ahnne. The woodcuts were not simply reprinted[4] from one edition to the next, but the themes were the same. The Old Testament had eighty-seven illustrations, including the Creation, Fall, Cain and Abel, the sacrifice of Isaac, and so on. The New Testament had twelve, chiefly for the Apocalypse. The Gospels had only one illustration each, the sign of the Evangelist plus accessory scenes exhibiting some point distinctive of the particular Gospel. Matthew was accompanied by the ancestors of Jesus, Mark by the resurrection, Luke by the Nativity, and John by the Trinity. And that was all.

This type persisted throughout all the editions of Luther's Bible printed during his lifetime. All these woodcuts have been

---

2. G. Millet, "Recherches sur l'iconographie de l'Évangile aux XIVe, XVe et XVIe siècles" (Paris 1916, reprint 1960), *Bibl. des Ec. franç. d'Athènes et de Rome*, fasc. 109.
3. Richard Muther, Die ältesten deutschen Bilder-Bibeln (München, 1883).
4. Paul Ahnne, "La Bible de Jean Grüninger 1485," *Les Livres illustrés Strasbourgeois de XVe siècle* (Strasbourg, 1952).

reproduced in a single volume by Schramm. The Revelation was the only book to be illustrated in the New Testament. The Gospels had the signs of the Evangelists[5] but without the accompanying scenes. In one instance Matthew was Luther himself and Luke, Melanchthon. Only in one edition was there a single woodcut on anything else in the life of Christ, namely, once a cut of the good Samaritan.

One cannot but wonder whether this reduction had any theological significance, because such a distribution of the illustrations meant an emphasis on the Creation, the Fall, and the judgment, since the weight of the illustrating was for Genesis and The Revelation. The Passion dropped out entirely and with it the resurrection. One cannot suppose that this was due to any diminution of interest because the Passion continued to be as central for the late Middle Ages as for the earlier centuries, and certainly for Luther it was the very core. As already noted Dürer devoted two series of woodcuts to the theme. Could it be that the Passionals, independently of the Bible, provided such a profusion of material that the Biblical accounts could leave the word to speak without the aid of the pictorial?

At any rate, whatever the explanation, this is the fact. But when we come to Virgil Solis' woodcuts in Veit Dietrich's epitome of Luther's Bible in 1562, this whole tradition is broken. He has, in all, seventy-six illustrations of the entire life of Christ: for Matthew, thirty-five; for Mark, two; for Luke, twenty; and for John, nineteen. Here are the themes in the order of their occurrence:

Matthew: The Evangelist, the Wise Men, slaughter of the innocents, baptism, temptation, call of the first disciples, the higher righteousness, "no man can serve two masters," storm at sea, dinner with a Pharisee, Jairus' daughter, John in prison, discourse on cross-bearing, the sower, the tares, Herodias, miracle of the loaves, Canaanite woman, Peter's confession, "suffer the little children," the kingdom is like a householder, the mother of the Zebedee, Palm Sunday, cleansing the Temple, marriage banquet, conspiracy of the Pharisees, abomination of desolation, Gethsemane, scourging, Pilate, Herod, *via crucis,* crucifixion, burial, empty tomb.

---

5. Albert Schramm, "Luther und die Bibel," *Die Illustrationen der Lutherbibel* (1923).

Mark: the Evangelist, curing of the dumb.

Luke: the Evangelist, Annunciation, Nativity, presentation, Simeon, boy Jesus in the Temple, sermon by the sea, paralytic, sinful woman, Good Samaritan, exorcism, the steward, Lazarus, the talents, Pharisee and publican, evil spirit, Zacchaeus, the Last Day, Last Supper, Emmaus.

John: sign of the Evangelist, John the Baptist, Cana, Nicodemus, centurion's son, Tiberias, attempt to stone Jesus, "I am the door," "I am the good shepherd," Lazarus, washing the disciples' feet, "In my Father's house," "My peace I give," "As my Father loveth me," the Comforter, "A little while and ye will not see me," "Whatever you ask of the Father," appearance to the disciples, Thomas.

How shall we account for this change? One is prompted to suggest that the clue lies in Luther's view that the Word of God is his self-disclosure in Christ. The Scripture is only the manger in which lay the baby Jesus, the Word. That in the Scripture is important which proclaims the Word regardless of the season of the year. Luther did not reject the Christian year, but much of his preaching consisted in the exposition of a Biblical book from beginning to end. Of all the Gospels, the chief for him was John and especially the discourses. These do not readily lend themselves to illustration, and yet they were illustrated by Virgil Solis. Even more significant was the way in which Luther treated the Biblical characters not as the costumed actors in a pageant but as persons agonizing and exulting over the mysteries of the faith. Such treatment tended to emancipate Biblical scenes from the liturgical framework and thus opened the path toward the profound individual delineations of Biblical characters in the painting of a Rembrandt.

Of very great help in the assembling of these excerpts has been the edition of Luther's sermons on the Gospels in five volumes by Erwin Mülhaupt.[6] He has translated all the Latin sermons into German and has rendered Luther's German into modern high

---

6. Erwin Mülhaupt and Ed. Ellwein, D. Martin Luthers Evangelienauslegung, 5 vols., third edition (Vandenhoeck & Ruprecht, Göttingen, 1960–1961), 2805 pp.

German. I have used this work as a guide to the originals in the Weimar edition on which my translations are based.

After this introduction was in type, I was informed by Professor François Bucher, of the department of Fine Arts at Brown University, that Mâle's observation as to the neglect in art of the public ministry of Jesus in the thirteenth century must be qualified in view of the recent discovery of several Bibles of that period copiously illustrated for the Gospels, though the generalization as to the emphasis still stands. This new material increases the puzzle as to why the printed German Bibles of the fifteenth and early sixteenth centuries should have been so parsimonious of illustration for the Gospels. The radicalism of Virgil Solis with reference to this tradition is not affected, though he would appear to have been reverting unwittingly to an earlier tradition. However, in his illustrating of the Johannine discourses he may have been entirely original. A definitive answer at this point calls for more extensive research in the medieval materials.

The brackets used in the following translations from Luther serve to set off explanatory remarks of the translator and summaries rather than translations of Luther.

R. H. B

1

The Coming of the Redeemer

The Prologue (John 1:1–14)

"In the beginning was the Word."

If the Word was before all creatures, and if they were created and came to be through it, then it is of a different being than the creatures, and it was not created or came to be as they. It must be eternal and have no beginning. When all things came into being, it was already there and is not to be comprised under creature and

time but hovers above time and creature, for through it time and creature come to be. This cannot be denied: what is not of time must be of eternity. That which has no beginning cannot be of time and what is not a creature must be God.

"In him was life."

The meaning of this passage in simple terms I take to be this: He who does not recognize and believe in Christ as truly God, who does not believe that he is the Word who was in the beginning with God through whom all things were made but regards him as a creature who had a beginning in time, is eternally lost and cannot have life.

"The light shineth in the darkness and the darkness comprehendeth it not."

The reference is to the natural light of reason, which is kindled by God and yet does not recognize, comprehend, or feel the light by which it is kindled. That is why it is in darkness and does not see the light from which it derives all of its own light. O that this reason were rooted out of my heart! How deeply it is ingrained! Not that it is false or improper, but it does not belong at this point in the Gospel and does not allow me to take these blessed and comforting words in their simple and plain meaning.

"In him was life; and the life was the light of men."

This is a light that shone, but nobody saw it. Therefore it had to be pointed out by an outward word and by John the Baptist. The Spirit did not show it. There had to be an outward man, an outward word, an outward finger. This is a thunderclap for the Spiritualists, who despise the outward word and wait upon the Spirit. John had to stand and say, "Behold the man!" This passage is an invincible weapon against those who would take away the outward preaching of the Word, who say it is of no use and attribute everything to the

Spirit. They make of none effect the preaching of John. If the Spirit does everything, why did he have to come and point out the light?

"John bare witness of him."

I believe the Evangelist is a heretic for rating John no higher than that. He makes him nothing more than a witness. The Evangelist should have given John a share in our salvation and should have let him teach us his ascetic deportment, but no, John's task is to point with his finger. And if John the Baptist was only a witness, what shall we say of St. Francis and the rest of the saints?

"As many as received him, to them gave he power to become the sons of God."

If you can believe on this man and on this light, I will tell you what you are: You have right and might and you may boast saying, "God is my father; I am his child." John wishes to express the unspeakable treasure belonging to believers. What an inexpressible gift it is to be a child of God! We cannot voice it with tongue or pen. Listen to John: "He is a child of God." What claim on a child of God can be made by Satan, kaiser, pope, devil, or death? What John is saying here is very simple yet inexpressible. To be a son of God is to be lord of sin, death, and hell. This text should be emblazoned in letters of gold.

We are made brothers of Christ and beloved children of God. All this is possessed by those who believe, only through faith. Some there are who amass gold and live in debauchery, but when grace ennobles them they too are glorified and are children of God. God sends his love through the Lord's Supper and through preaching. Faith gives a child not as a painter depicts, but a child born of God, that is begotten and born anew through the Holy Ghost.

"And John bare record, saying, I saw the Spirit descending from heaven."

Before the coming of Christ the heaven was tightly closed, and the devil reigned mightily. But in Christ and through Christ the heaven is opened again, and we can hear the Heavenly Father talking with us, and the dear angels hover over us. These words, "Thou art my beloved Son," are still spoken to us always by the Father and will be until the Judgment Day, and heaven will never be closed. If you come to Baptism and receive the Lord's Supper and absolution, heaven is open and the voice of the Father in heaven is heard.

The Genealogies (Matt. 1:1–17)

Ever since the time of the Gospel there has been perplexity as to why Matthew and Luke should present discrepant genealogies of Jesus. And what is more serious is that to prove the Davidic descent they should trace the line through Joseph, who was not his father, rather than through Mary, who was his mother. The Jews and after them Julian the Apostate, and many others, ancient and modern, have in consequence declared our faith to be false, uncertain, or at least utterly obscure. But the primary point is whether Jesus was the Messiah. Matthew begins his Gospel with the words, "The generation of Jesus Christ, the son of David." If then he was the Christ, that is the Messiah, the son of David, his mother must have been of the house of David.

The Annunciation (Luke 1:26–38)

Mary was a poor maid. To be sure, she was of the house of David, but the priests had arrogated power to themselves until the house of David had fallen into such disrepute that to expect a king from the tree of Jesse [David's father] was like looking for a flower from a shriveled, rotten, old root. Mary was a waif.

The story that Joachim and Anna divided their substance into three portions and gave her one is pure fable. She was perhaps a poor orphan and despised, because she said of herself that God "regarded the low estate of his handmaiden." To this poor maid the marvelous announcement was given that she should be the mother of the Most High, who would be called a Son of God. He would be a king and of his Kingdom there would be no end. She might well have said, "Who am I, little worm, that I should give birth to a king?" She might have doubted, but she shut her eyes and trusted in God that he is powerful and can bring all things to pass, though reason and all creatures be against it. Because she believed, the word of the angel was fulfilled in her. At first she held back, and said, "How shall this be, seeing I

know not a man?" She too was flesh and blood. Therefore the angel reassured her, "The Holy Ghost shall come upon thee, and the power of the Highest shall overshadow thee. . . . And, behold, thy cousin Elizabeth, she hath also conceived a son in her old age."

[Even so we are abashed because God offers us so much.] When we come to die nature and the devil confront us with the overflowing abundance of the gifts of God, and we recoil at the thought that to those who believe, Christ is Lord of sin, death, and hell and that we thereby are fellow heirs with him. We say: "We are poor and miserable. Who are we that we should live forever in heaven? We are not fit to receive such great gifts." Then the heart falters. One must be very wise not to let oneself be dismayed. Christ comforted his disciples saying, "Fear not, little flock, for it is the Father's good pleasure to give you the Kingdom."

The angel quickens us to believe that the child will be a mighty king and will be called the son of the Highest. The mightier we make this king the more will our faith be strengthened if we believe that he is so mighty. There are some who believe that Christ is Lord, but not that he is Lord of all things. They do not believe that Christ is Lord of the enemy. When such men are beleaguered they leap to violence and to defend themselves. They really do not believe. If they did, they would say: "Whom then shall I fear? God is my Father and Lord, nothing will happen to me without his will." When we believe, we fear no man.

The angel Gabriel might have gone to the daughter of Caiaphas, rich, fair, and clad in gold-embroidered raiment. Instead he went to Mary, whose name means bitterness in view of the bitter plight of her people, like that of our own today.

Benedict and Bernhard saw here three miracles: the first, that God became man; the second, that a virgin was a mother; and the third, that the heart of man should believe this.

Really the virgin birth is not such a great miracle, because Jesus was made out of flesh and blood. This was not so extraordinary as making Adam out of mud and Eve out of a rib, but we do not regard any of these as miraculous because we have heard about them so often. I do not suppose Adam and Eve believed their creation to

have been miraculous. We do not believe that our own births are miraculous. Where in the seed is the material for eyes and teeth and nails? So all God's works are incredible. Mary believed, and yet she overlooked the greater miracle that her child would be the Son of God. She did not ask how that could be and how his Kingdom could be without end. She forgot all this. Her thought centered on herself, and she asked only how *she* could conceive, though the other was more marvelous. It is only a little miracle for God to make a virgin conceive, but to create a man who is also eternal, that is a great miracle.

Such miracles we should take to ourselves for our comfort. It is a great consolation for us that divine majesty became flesh and blood, and an even greater consolation if we can believe that this happened for *us*. We merely talk, but if a prince for my sake were to go to prison, should I not see he loved me and should I not be beside myself? Such an outward thing is nothing compared with what God, who has all things in his hand, has done. Surely if one believed this, the heart would break in a thousand pieces for very joy.

The Visitation (Luke 1:39–56)

When Mary heard that her cousin Elizabeth was with child, she set out to help her. Mary was of royal lineage and was to be the true, natural mother of God. Yet she set out on foot on a journey of two or three days to do maid service for Elizabeth. Shame on all of us for our pride! No peasant and no townsman of good family among us would stoop so far. If one of us is descended from a noble or a prince, there is no end of bragging. Yet no queen of the Romans or empress could be compared with Mary. What honor is there in the world to be compared with her honor, and she was of royal seed! She might well have said: "Why should I go to help that priest's old lady? It is beneath me, for I am of David's house, and I am carrying the Son of God. The angels should take me in a chariot of gold with wheels studded with jewels." She was descended from the noblest stock, and spiritually she was God's daughter. Nevertheless she went on foot to visit her cousin. Though she was carrying the Son of God, she was willing to be a maid. All the maids among us should be proud of this – Mary was one of them.

"When Elizabeth heard the salutation of Mary, the babe leaped in her womb."

John knew before his mother that Mary was carrying the Savior. This shows that the Baptists are wrong when they say that babies should not be baptized because they do not have their full five senses and have not arrived at the age of reason. John had none of his five senses, let alone reason, but God and the Holy Spirit have reason enough.

When John leaped in the womb, then his mother perceived what she had not discerned by the sight of the eyes, for Mary's condition was not yet evident.

Elizabeth saw beyond appearance like Abel who saw the fire that consumed the sacrifice, and faith discerned behind the fire the mercy of God.

Elizabeth was then so overcome that she did not thank Mary, nor did she greet her with "*Liebe Maria*" but said instead: "Blessed art thou among women, and blessed is the fruit of thy womb. And whence is this to me, that the mother of my Lord should come to me?" "Why has this honor come to me, for I am a poor, miserable, wrinkled, despised, old woman. Why didn't you go to the wife of Annas the high priest or of Caiaphas?" Elizabeth forgot that Mary was of royal blood and called her only mother and the mother of the Lord. One humility confronted another. Mary humbled herself, and Elizabeth considered herself unworthy to have her come, though she was very pleased. Then she explained why she had forgotten to welcome her and thanked her because at her word the babe leaped in her womb. And then she added, "Blessed is she that hath believed."

In Mary and Elizabeth we see how mighty a thing is genuine faith, for it changes a man in soul and body. Elizabeth had become another woman full of inexpressible joy. Her body and tongue were so joyous that she became a prophetess. She was also filled with such assurance that were the world with devils filled she would have trembled not for them. So also Mary. Such a change happens when faith is in the heart, and even if now, where it does not yet appear what we shall be, faith does this for flesh and blood addicted to sin, how will it be when we see what now we believe and when that shall be revealed which now is hidden? Such a change takes place now, where we only hear about God. There we shall find even greater righteousness, assurance, and peace, and we shall be utterly drowned in sheer joy and love eternal.

Elizabeth had said to Mary, "Blessed art thou among women," and Mary accepted this statement and responded: "My soul doth magnify the Lord, and my spirit hath rejoiced in God my Savior. For he hath regarded the low estate of his handmaiden: For, behold, from henceforth all generations shall call me blessed." Was that not pride for a young girl? No, there is no humility in denying the gifts which God has given. If somebody said I have hands, should I humble myself and say, "I beg your pardon, they are hoofs"?

One should admit frankly what one is: I am learned; I know how to study; I am devout; I am no adulterer; or I am a princess; I am a countess; I have ten gulden; and so on. One should not deny what God has given, such as gold and goods, since all is his gift. The sun does not say that it is black. The tree does not say, "I bear no apples, pears, or grapes." That is not humility, but if you have gifts you should say, "These gifts are from God; I did not confer them upon myself." One should not be puffed up on their account. If someone else does not have the gifts I have, then he has others. If I exalt my gifts and despise another's, that is pride. The sun does not vaunt himself, though more fair than the earth and the trees, but says, "Although, tree, you do not shine, I will not despise you, for you are green and I will help you to be green." That is what we all should do and that is what Mary did here.

She did not lord it over Elizabeth, but she waited on her and brought her some soup and gave John a bath. This is the second grade of humility; namely, not to despise those who have lesser gifts. That is what Christ did. He was the Lord and on equality with God, but he emptied himself of all lordship and did not tread us under his feet, but he said: "Ye call me Master and Lord: and ye say well; for so I am. If I then, your Lord and Master, have washed your feet; ye also ought to wash one another's feet" (John 13:13–14).

The Magnificat (Luke 1:46–55)

Mary sang, "My soul doth magnify the Lord"-not herself, but the Lord. She was Queen of Queens, Virgin of Virgins, Mother of Mothers, but she despised no man. "True it is," she said, "I am blessed, but I do not magnify myself, my soul doth magnify the Lord. What I am, I am through his grace, which he has bestowed upon me, unworthy as I am." Here we have the highest joy and still humility; honor and subjection not only toward God but also toward men.

"My spirit bath rejoiced in God my Savior. For he hath regarded the low estate of his handmaiden."

Mary was of low estate, as we have seen. She was a waif. God has to abase before he can exalt. Mary had to suffer more than once. At the end, she saw her son crucified. How she must have suffered when she heard him reviled as he preached! What he suffered, she also suffered. This is not to say that she had not sweet moments, but there were alternate periods of bitterness; and how grievous it must have been for her to fall under the suspicion of her husband, who was minded to put her away!

In Latin the expression "low estate" was translated *humilitas*, as if Mary were saying that God had exalted her humility, but if she had been conscious of her humility, it would not have been humility. If she had known she was humble, she would have been proud. Humility is so tender and precious that it cannot look upon itself. To behold humility is to look upon the face of God.

Mary sang, "He that is mighty hath done for me great things." She did not deny what he had done. She declared that he was mighty who could do such things, and that is very true. Who among men is mighty enough to cause a virgin to bear a son? Man has not the power to guarantee that one will be in health for a day, to make a grain of wheat sprout from the earth, or to bring down a drop of dew from heaven. Of no moment in our lives are we certain; nothing is weaker than man.

Mary praised God because he had done for her great things.

Today there are many who do not praise God's goodness because they do not have as much by way of good things as Saint Peter or a saint or somebody else on earth. They think that if they had as much, then they also would praise God and love him. They despise and do not recognize the gifts with which they have been showered, such as body, life, reason, goods, honor, friends, and the services of the sun and of all creatures. If they had all the gifts of Mary, they would not see therein the hand of God, nor praise him. They look at those above them instead of those below. Were they to do the latter, they would perchance see so many who do not have as much as they and yet are content with God and praise him. The bird sings and is happy with what he has and does not grumble because he cannot read. The dog jumps up joyously and is content although he is not endowed with reason. All the animals are content and serve God with love and praise. Only the evil, envious eye of man is insatiable.

We read that at the time of the Council of Constance a cardinal went for a ride in a field and saw there a peasant weeping. The cardinal, being a kind man, did not wish to ride by, and stopped to comfort the man. The peasant wept for a long time and would say nothing, so that the cardinal worried about him. Then the peasant pointed to a toad and said, "I am weeping because God has made me such a fine creature and not ugly like that toad, and yet I have never acknowledged his gift with thanks and praise." Then the cardinal was so smitten that he fell from his horse and had to be carried into a house. When he regained his senses he said, "O Saint Augustine, how well have you said, 'The unlettered rise up and take heaven before us and we with all our skills wallow in flesh and blood'!"

"Holy is his name."

Mary ascribed everything to God. She did not proclaim that she was to be God's mother, and after leaving Elizabeth, she returned to Nazareth and went about her housework just as before, milked the cow, cooked, washed the dishes, swept, doing the little things, the despised tasks of the maid and the housemother, as if all the inexpressible gifts and graces were nothing. Among the women of the neighborhood she was no more esteemed than before and did not ask to be anything but one among the common folk. What a simple and pure heart!

"His mercy is on them that fear him."

Those who fear him are those who recognize his goodness and all his gifts and yet are ready in an hour to let everything go if it be his will. If that happens, will you scream, rage, rave, and strangle the world because your right has been violated? Leave all to God.

But does that mean that the lord of the land should not protect his people? Shall he be quiet and let anything happen? By no means. Civil rulers are obligated to protect subjects, for they bear the sword in order to keep the peace. They would gladly let the sword rust if God had not commanded them to punish the wicked. However, the protection should not create a greater evil. There is no point in taking a spoon as compensation because a platter has been broken. It is sorry protection to imperil a city for the sake of one man or to endanger a country for the sake of a castle. A knight robs a citizen and to punish the wrong you bring out an army and lay waste the land. Similarly a subject should be ready to suffer rather than ask that on his account all others be brought into peril.

"He hath showed strength with his arm."

God's arm is directly against the proud. But we are of so little faith that we strike with the fist. If we do not feel the arm of God, we say, "It is all over with us, and the enemy has won." This we say because we do not know God, nor his mercy, nor his arm, because he must and will be known only through faith.

Man feels nothing and sees nothing, but man believes. Reason cannot grasp this, but faith is sure and even more sure than by the sight of the eyes. We must learn the nature of faith. So will it be in the hour of death. Nature will crumble, but I will say with the psalmist, "I will both lay me down in peace, and sleep: for thou, Lord, only makest me dwell in safety" (Ps. 4:8).

"He hath put down the mighty from their seats."

Correct, but he does not overturn the seats. So long as the world lasts there will have to be magistracy, government, force, and seats. The princes must be humble because God casts down the tyrants from their seats, but he leaves the seats.

"He hath filled the hungry with good things."

It is not possible that God should allow one who trusts in him to die of hunger, but we are to remember that God cannot fill us before we are hungry. We have to experience hunger and want in order to know that only God can help us. How can God fill before he makes hungry? How can he exalt before he makes low? And conversely, how can he abase unless first he lifts up? And how can he make poor save him who has been made rich?

"He bath holpen his servant Israel."

The word "service," related to the word "servant," has been much abused. We talk about the church service, and we have reference to the ringing of bells in a church of wood or stone, to the burning of incense, the flames of the candles, the mumbling of the liturgy, the gold and silk and jewels in the vestments, the chalice, the monstrance, the organ and images, processions and cloisters, and above all, the babbling and the saying of rosaries. This is called the church service.

"To Abraham, and to his seed for ever."

In view of this verse we should not be so unkind to the Jews because there may be among them future Christians.

The Boyhood of Jesus (Luke 2:39–40)

At Nazareth, Jesus helped his father, Joseph, build houses. Joseph was a carpenter. What, then, will the people of Nazareth say on the last day when they see Christ? They will say: "Lord, did you not help build my house? How did you come to such glory?" It is a great glory to know that for our sakes Christ humbled himself and for our sakes so long hid his majesty. First, he lay in a cradle and was nourished by milk, then he went into exile and on his return helped his father. He will often have gone to fetch bread and water for his mother, and she will have said to him: "Laddie, where have you been? Could you not stay home?" I am not offended [says Luther] by such weakness and littleness. It is great wisdom.

The Boy Jesus Lost in the Temple (Luke 2:41–52)

Human reason would undoubtedly like to teach God a lesson that he should not have allowed his son to be shamefully treated as a thief and a murderer. Christ should not have had to shed his blood, but all angels should have borne him up upon their wings, while kings and lords should have bowed down before him. But Christ had to suffer and the Gospel shows that his dear mother also seldom experienced the lovely and joyous but for the

most part endured sheer sorrow and anxiety according to the prophecy of Simeon in order that she might be an example to all Christendom. The first instance is that at Bethlehem there was no room for her in the inn and the second that she had to flee with her child into Egypt. But not the least of her sorrow was that Christ lost himself from her in the Temple, and she had to search so long without finding him. She was so frightened and troubled as nearly to collapse, as she herself said, "Thy father and I have sought thee sorrowing." Let us think for a moment what a state she must have been in. Every father and mother will understand what a frightful worry it is when a dear child disappears without being noticed, and they do not know but that he may be lost. If it lasts only an hour, what sadness, wailing, and crying, with no comfort, no eating, drinking, sleeping, or peace and such anxiety that they would rather be dead! And how much worse it is when this lasts a whole day, and a whole night or longer, when every hour is not a year in length but a hundred!

Look now at this mother having lost a son who was to her as no son ever was to another, because she was his mother without a human father. He was God's true son, and God had specially entrusted him to her. She had until then taken infinite pains. Now he was so far grown as to be to her a great comfort. What it must have been to lose him suddenly when she thought him old enough to be let out of her sight! And he was missing not an hour or two, not a day and a night, but three whole days, so that she could not but think she had lost him forever. Who can say or imagine how her mother's heart was rent during those three whole days? It is a wonder that she could live through such anguish.

Her pain was the greater because she could not regard his loss as an accident for which she was not to blame. This smote her conscience. She must have reflected that God had entrusted this child to her and made her solely responsible. This thought must have thundered in her heart: "See, you have lost this child. It is all your fault because you should have looked after the lad and not let him for a moment out of your sight. What will you say to God that you did not look out for him better? You do not deserve to be his mother any more. You deserve to be damned in the sight of all men because so great honor was done to you in that you were chosen to be his mother." What sin could compare with this—that she had done badly by God's Son and the Savior of the world! If God had decided to take him back to heaven, she would be the cause that the world would not be saved. She must have thought of all this and much more, and her heart was sore affrighted. Conscience is a tender thing, and she had a very tender heart and conscience.

This is the hardest and deepest trial with which God sometimes afflicts his saints. It is called the withdrawal of grace. That is when the heart of man feels that God has withdrawn his favor and when man turns to him there is nought but wrath and terror. Not everyone knows such trials, and no one understands save he who has experienced them. It takes strong spirits to come through to the end. This example is given us that we may learn how to endure and be solaced in our trials.

2

Beginnings of the Ministry

The Feast of Epiphany and the Baptism (Matt. 3:13–17)

On Epiphany, we commemorate the baptism of Jesus, the appearance of the star, the miracle at Cana, and the coming of the three kings. Unfortunately, the first item has been forgotten and the fourth has stolen the day. The three kings are supposed to be buried at Cologne and over their remains a magnificent church has been reared. They are vastly more rich dead than ever they were alive. The names Caspar, Melchior, and Balthasar have been given to them. Call them that if you like. The main point is that on this day we should not forget the baptism of Jesus. As for the bones of these kings, I have seen them, and I don't know whether they are the bones of kings or peasants. It is amazing that in matters of business no peasant is so dumb as not to demand a receipt, but in matters of faith we believe incredible nonsense without any evidence. Who knows whether these so-called kings were three and who knows who they were? Perhaps Turks.

Let us now turn to the baptism. At that time Jesus came from Galilee to Jordan. The baptism of Jesus is the beginning of the New Testament. The Lord here assumed his office. This was the occasion when he took his doctor's degree and received his doctor's barret. John the Baptist on this occasion heard a voice and saw a dove. This is recorded for the sake of you and me. Jesus had no need for a voice or a dove. This revelation was for my comfort because unless I can see and hear, it is of no use to me. God gave his stamp of approval to Jesus at the baptism in the words, "This is my beloved Son." If only men had listened solely to this teacher, the three kings would never have gone to Cologne, and we should not have been addicted to superstitions.

Jesus came to be baptized, but John said to him no, rather he should be baptized by Jesus. John certainly exceeded all men in good works. He ate no meat and lived on wild honey and was clothed in coarse camel's hair with a leathern girdle. He had no wife, lived in the wilderness, and above all, he preached. Yet, he despised all his austerities and said, "I am nothing." What shall we make of this? Was he not as good as a Carthusian? Was he not as chaste as a virgin? as obedient as a monk? Yet he said to Jesus: "Shall I baptize thee? Shall I not rather be baptized by thee?" If we listen to John, all of us, the worldly wise and the mighty, we shall all be put to shame. John confessed that he was a sinner. . . . If Christ were to come to Rome, they would say to him: "Shall we be baptized by thee? Come and be baptized by us." But John demurred. Jesus, however, said to him, "Let it be." Similarly, we would be willing to eat only fish on Friday to please the pope provided he did not make the requirement into an article of faith.

The Temptations (Matt. 4:1–11)

"Then was Jesus led up of the Spirit into the wilderness to be tempted of the devil."

The order of Christ's temptations cannot be determined with precision. Matthew has one order and Luke another. For the purpose of preaching, the order of Luke is to be preferred. He has the devil first tempt Christ with reference to his need. [He is hungry.] Next he is tempted with reference to his resources. [Let him throw himself from the pinnacle of the temple.] The third temptation is by way of lies and illusions. [He is promised the kingdoms of the earth.] Matthew changes the order because, as a matter of fact, the devil observes no order in temptations. He breaks into the garden wherever the fence is lowest. He may begin with the first temptation and jump to the second and after ten days come back to the first.

The story of the temptations is read at the beginning of the Lenten fast. But this is perfect nonsense. No one can go forty days and forty nights with absolutely nothing to eat. The worst of it is that our fasts are treated as good works. They do great harm to pregnant women and sickly persons who because of them have lost their lives. In any case, no one should impose trials upon himself but should wait for the Spirit. We shall have trials enough without hunting after them. We read that Jesus was driven into the wilderness by the Spirit and not that he went of his own accord.

The wilderness signifies to be abandoned by God, angels, men, and all creatures.

The devil then tempts Christ as to his belly that he should no longer trust in God's provision: "If thou be the Son of God, command that these stones be made bread!"

It is as if he would say: "Yes, just leave it to God and do not bake any more bread. Sit back and wait until a roast chicken jumps into your mouth; you say that you have a God who looks after you; where is your Heavenly Father who looks after you? . . . Eat and drink now from your faith, and let's see how fat you will grow. ... A fine son of God you are! And what a Father you have who never so much as sends you a crust! . . . Can you go on believing that you are his Son and he is your Father?"

With such thoughts [adds Luther] the devil tempts God's children, and Christ assuredly felt them, for although he was pure and without sin as we are not, at the same time he was no log or stone.

Christ then replies: "Man lives not by bread alone. . . . This life which you tell me that I shall lose by dying does not depend on bread. When you have bread, you don't live from it; and he who has none does not die of hunger. This is plain to the eye in the case of a man who amasses thousands and in a twinkling they are gone. God can turn them to dust, so that the man and his children must beg. But what, then, keeps us alive? It is God's word. With out this your goods vanish. Bread does not feed you, nor clothes cover and adorn. We live from the word and the blessing that lies therein."

The second temptation is that he should throw himself down from the pinnacle of the Temple. There was absolutely no need to jump because there were perfectly good stairs. Note how the devil shifted his tack. Since Christ could not be tempted as to his

belly, the devil says: "Very well, you wish to be entirely spiritual. May I help you?" He quotes Scripture: "God will give his angels charge over you lest you dash your foot against a stone." (Ps. 91:11.) But the rascal omits the next verse: "He will keep you in all your ways." That is to say, the ways which God has commanded. The temptation to go beyond these commands does not occur very often in worldly things, though there are some who embark on foolhardy wars, and none is so easily drowned as a good swimmer nor killed as an expert mountain climber.

But God has given his angels charge over you only if you stay in the way appointed. If you try to swim the Elbe, the angels won't look after you. If you are a married man, a wife, or a child, the angels will be there if you do your duty and do not go trotting off to Rome. The same applies to bishops and preachers. If they preach the gospel, the angels are their guardians.

Note that the first temptation occurred in the wilderness, the second in the Temple. The first arose from a lack of life's necessities, the second from the very abundance of God's promises.

The third has to do with honor and power. If the devil cannot win with poverty and misery, he tries riches, favor, honor, and power.

Observe that the kingdoms of the world over which Satan offered to give Christ command are exactly those over which the pope claims dominion. The papal tiara in three layers signifies his lordship over the three parts, Europe, Africa, and Asia. The pope's flatterers claim that he is Lord of the whole, but Christ's response to this temptation was "Get thee behind me, Satan."

The Call of the First Disciples: of Peter and Andrew, who Left their Nets, and James and John, who Left their Boat and their Father (Matt. 4:18–22)

They left not only their nets but also their boats. One might say that they did not leave much, but people who talk in that fashion have not tried themselves out to see whether they could give up a florin. To be sure, it would not have been much to leave the nets and the boats if that were all that they had left, but these were their livelihood. They were giving up everything that boat and nets can bring in. What fisherman would give up a boat unless he had no use for it any more? To forsake everything in this way for Christ is what is meant by taking the cross. The nets mean everything with which goods are gained. The boat means the soul or passion of the will and heart with which all these goods are brought to land. The nets, then, are the means and arts for acquiring gain, riches, enjoyment, honor, and dignity. For these are the fruits of man's fishing and when they are won then men take them as in a ship over the sea to enjoy them. To leave the boat means to renounce passionate attachment to all this and the desire to enjoy it. For so long as the heart is attached to these physical and visible things, it cannot live in faith. To take the cross and leave all things in the word of faith is a hard thing, for the cross kills the passionate craving for these things and makes one willing to renounce them, but faith sustains the mortified by other means neither seen nor experienced.

The Marriage at Cana (John 2:1–11)

"The mother of Jesus saith unto him, They have no wine. Jesus saith unto her, Woman, what have I to do with thee?"

How roughly Jesus rebuked the humble remark of his mother, who was concerned about the guests! Just see what this did to faith. What was there to believe in? Utter nothingness and darkness—no help in sight—God estranged and hostile—nothing whatever left! This is what happens to us when in our consciences we feel sin and the lack of righteousness and when in the hour of death we feel life slipping and the horror of hell grips us and the hope of blessedness fades. Then in all humility we ask and knock, beg and seek, that we may be delivered from sin, death, and despair. But Christ acts as if sin would win and death remain and hell never cease, just as he treated his mother and by his rebuff made her distress greater than it had been before. At such a time it seems as if all is lost. Faith then is sorely assailed, but see what his mother does and learn from her. No matter how gruff he sounded she would not believe that he was angry and ill-disposed. Had the mother allowed herself to be repelled by these harsh words she would have done nothing, but when she told the servants to do what he said, she showed that she had surmounted the rebuff and expected from him only sheer kindness. From this we learn that we should regard God as kind and gracious even though all our senses and feeling indicate the contrary. Then feeling is killed and the old man destroyed to be replaced simply by faith in God's goodness.

The reason why Christ did say this to his mother was to show that in God's service we are not to follow father and mother. "He who does the will of my Father in heaven is my brother and sister and mother."

Incidentally, he wanted to show that in matters of salvation, we are not to run to the Virgin Mary.

Then he turned the water into wine. He did not dampen the conviviality of the wedding. He had no objection to the decoration and to the joviality, the eating and the drinking. His objection was only to guzzling and swilling like swine. He does not turn water into wine for that kind. But is it not a sin to pipe and dance at a wedding since so much sin in derived from dancing? Whether the Jews danced at weddings I do not know, but since it is the custom in our country I am of no mind to condemn it but only to reprove excess.

Since marriage is ordained of God and honored by Christ, everyone should know that it is dear to God and one should cheerfully endure whatever hardship is entailed even though it were ten times harder.

Had not our Lord thus hallowed matrimony, I believe it would have been totally despised. Those who believe that marriage is ordained of God have joy in the Lord because they know that the Lord has joy in it. They know this: It is pleasing to God that I have a wife. There is no greater joy of the heart than this assurance that in marriage God smiles graciously upon us.

When the wine gave out and they did not have any beer, the bridegroom stood there like a poor beggar. This shows that marriage has its trials, but Christ by the miracle shows that he will fill up whatever is lacking in marriage. He turns water into wine as if he would say: "Do you have to drink water, that is, do you have trouble in the outward man and is it bitter? See then, I will make it sweet and turn the water into wine. I will not pour out the water, it will have to stay, but I will perfect it. I will not take the vexation out of marriage, I may even increase it, but it will turn out wonderfully as they alone know who have experienced it." God's Word makes water into wine, and a bitter marriage becomes a joy.

But if you get married because you think you will be all buoyed up, you'll get something more than you bargained for. Marriage is

Beginnings of the Ministry

more a matter of waking than of sleeping. God give you a wife you can live with. No matter how good-looking she is, the wine won't last long unless some new wine comes out of the water. Namely, that God puts into your heart to regard your wife as a precious treasure and vice versa and you will not get this through a great fortune, house, castle, or reputation. No, if God does not give you

another wine, you will be quarreling and saying, "You're not good enough for me." Who will help here? There may be two handsome persons and still neither joy nor love. The devil is there; the jug is empty. The mother must come and say, "They have no wine," and Christ must make the water into wine. If you are having trouble in your marriage, say to yourself, "God ordained this estate; it pleases him." He who wants fire will have to put up with some smoke. You can't have dancing all the time. Say to yourself, "In this estate I can live with a good conscience"; this is more than a monk can say, for whenever did Christ command, "Tonsure me a monk"? Therefore if you think you are a captive in marriage, be consoled and joyful and let the wife say: "When my husband embraces me, God embraces me. I may have a hard time, but my estate is pleasing to God." And this is more than a pope, bishop, or pilgrim can say.

When you are getting married take counsel of parents and friends. Remember that any girl can sleep. Pick one who is some good when she is awake. Physical attraction soon passes. There has got to be something more than that. You must be ready to care for each other, bring up children, endure adversity, and stand by each other in the pest. Young people should not make secret engagements, and parents should not prevent their children from getting married. A father who does that is a tyrant and a very devil, and if the magistrate won't help you against such a father, do for yourself what you can.

Nicodemus (John 3:1–15)

Nicodemus is an example of nature that even when most enlightened, is nevertheless blind. One has to destroy reason and enter into the birth. Abraham had a son through whom his seed should be as the stars in heaven. And then God told him to kill his son. If Abraham had listened to reason, he would have said: "See, God has promised me a son through whom my seed shall be increased, and now he tells me to sacrifice this son. This is not of God but rather of the devil." But Abraham destroyed reason, crawled out of his old skin and into God, believed in him, and became a new man. Then came the call of the angel, "No, no, Abraham!" But Abraham could not know that God would do this. In his heart he had already killed his son.

This spiritual birth begins in baptism. He is newborn who says: "My soul is in God's hand. As in the past, so in the days to come, he will marvelously feed and sustain me. When we die we must leave this world and do not know where we are going. The inn is not ready. Anxiety begins to assail. This is the true hell, fear, horror, and despair. But when I am newborn, I shut my eyes and say: 'O God, my soul is in thy hand. Thou hast upheld me, I know not how; and though for the future I know not, this alone I know, that my soul is in thy hand and thou wilt help.' "

Nicodemus was puzzled and asked, "How can a man when he is old be born again?" Christ tells him that that is precisely

Beginnings of the Ministry

what must happen. We must become nothing if we would see God. Only Christ opens the gate of grace, not I. That is why this experience is called a new birth of the Spirit, for it is not born of nature. To Nicodemus he says: "Are you a ruler of Israel, and do not understand this? You must be changed from the very ground of your being." Reason cannot understand how a man that is old can be born again. Reason cannot understand how the wind bloweth where it listeth, neither can you understand that you must become nothing. You are a respectable man, and no one can reproach you, but you do not consider that you are a reprobate. You sit in the Sanhedrin. You have a wife, and you are a doctor. Does all this count for nothing? In the eyes of the world it is something but not in the eyes of God. The Spirit must be your teacher.

"No man hath ascended up to heaven, but he that came down from heaven."

This text does not mean that Christ is located in heaven and ascends and descends. The ascension of Christ and of all Christians is spiritual and not attached to any place. If I believe, I live in God. I am above all creatures, the devil and every power, but nobody sees it. One cannot recognize a Christian by an outward sign. He has no nose but is like the wind of which I know not whence it blows. Like Christ, we are physically subject to all, but spiritually above all creatures. Nothing can hurt our souls whether on earth or in heaven.

What works contribute to this new birth? Nothing. To be born again I must suffer and be still that my Father and Creator may fashion me. Otherwise God is not God alone.

The Woman at the Well (John 4:1–14)

"Give me to drink."

Strange it is that Christ on earth had to beg a cup of cold water from a woman. This is to let us know that while Christ was on earth he was hungry and thirsty, poor and naked, and died on the cross. Why did he not stay in heaven since he was lord of all and did not need to suffer want and hunger? But as soon as he came into the world, which is the devil's kingdom, and as soon as he came to his own children, he did not have a drink of cold water and he had to die on the cross for thirst, when vinegar and myrrh were given to him to drink. To the woman he said, "Give me to drink." She wondered that he a Jew should ask a drink from her, a Samaritan and a woman. He did not leave off but said to her graciously: "Dear daughter, it is true that I ask for a drink because I am tired and in need, but I am interested in something else. I seek you Samaritans." Then he went on to give her a wonderful word about the water of life.

The Woman Who was a Sinner, Who Washed the Master's Feet (Luke 7:36–50)

Now when Jesus was reproached for allowing this woman to show him attention, he turned on the Pharisee and said: "You gave me no water to wash my hands, a small enough service, but you were too proud. This woman, whose sins I have forgiven, had neither water

Beginnings of the Ministry

nor oil, but the tears of her eyes has she used and washed not my hands, but the lowest members, my feet. You gave me no towel. She had none of silk, but she used her braids, her best adornment, not to dry my face or my neck but my feet. You gave me no kiss on hand, cheek, or mouth (that was the custom then as today in North Germany). You could have kissed me in accord with the custom of the country, but you did not kiss because you are such a proud donkey. She has fallen on her knees and kissed my feet. Guests are honored with water of lavender or rose. You did not think of this, but she has brought balsam and spikenard, very costly, and has poured this on my soiled feet, which you did not notice."

One sees that Christ's office calls both for forgiveness and reproof. It was a sin of the flesh he forgave, a sin of the spirit he reproved.

The Beheading of John the Baptist (Mark 6:14–29)

John's ministry will scarcely have lasted over two years. How meanly his end comported with the proclamation of the angel about him and the word of the Master that none greater than John was born of woman! After such a prodigious announcement so brief and paltry a

labor! For two years he preached repentance and then lost his head. This superb man, lauded by an angel and by the Lord Christ, must suffer a shameful death because of an adulteress. Secretly, in prison he was killed, and his head brought to the hussy in her chamber. When Christ heard of it, he acted as if he were unmoved. He did not curse or weep. He did nothing. With perfect right he might have brought down thunder and lightning on the dance. Who would follow Christ when he allowed his greatest saint to be executed and did nothing? It is said that the heathen burned John's bones and reduced him to ashes. The nuns at Rome claim they have his heart, but we know better. Others say they have the finger with which he pointed at Christ. We should reflect that this man so heralded perished so miserably that nothing of him can be found. What are our troubles and despondencies compared to this? But the wrath of God came upon this people which killed the prophets. Forty years after John's death, the Temple was in ruins. God first removes his saints that they may not live to see hell-fire raining from heaven.

3

The Sermon on the Mount

(Matt., chapters 5 to 7)

The Ethic

The injunctions of the Sermon on the Mount, not to avenge oneself, not to go to law, to give one's cloak, to turn the other cheek, to go the second mile, to resist not evil, to love enemies, etc.—all these are not counsels but precepts [that is, they are not exhortations addressed to those who aspire to perfection but commands binding upon all Christians].

But the prohibition of anger does not apply to the magistrate. He must be angry. Wrath is a virtue with magistrates and all Christians who are in positions of authority such as parents.

The sword is no foxtail or a rosary, but a sharp instrument that God has given to the judge and the anger is not his but God's. He is moved by the compunction of charity and mercy while at the same time administering God's wrath. The same is true in things spiritual, as when the apostles were wrathful, The anger instilled by the Holy Ghost, as when the Pharisee is branded a hypocrite in danger of judgment and hell, is that not reviling?

The two jurisdictions, civil and spiritual, must be distinguished and both upheld—the one induces piety, the other keeps the peace. Neither suffices without the other. Without Christ's spiritual rule no one can be approved in God's eyes simply through the civil power. Where only civil government and law obtain, there one will find hypocrisy, because without the Holy Spirit in the heart, no one can be really godly, no matter how fine his works appear. But if only the spiritual administration rules over land and people, then villainy will break out because the world cannot accept spiritual jurisdiction or understand it.

The Beatitudes

"Blessed are the poor." Matthew adds, "in spirit." The Jews supposed that only the good would possess the land flowing with milk and honey and would be blessed through affluence, but Christ here reverses the order and reduces to poverty those who truly would be rich with God, just as he humbles those who wish to be exalted and kills those who seek to be saved.

"Blessed are the meek." Not through warring but through gentleness shall man be lord over the goods of the earth.

"Blessed are they that mourn." In bearing adversity there is confidence and joy.

"Blessed are they that hunger and thirst after righteousness." Not through fasting.

"Blessed are the merciful." This falls into three parts. (1) Give to him that asks. (2) Repulse not him that would borrow. (3) If anyone would take thy coat, give him thy cloak also.

"Blessed are the pure in heart, for they shall see God." There are those who seek to penetrate the immensities and to see God. One ought rather to sink into the depths and seek to find God among the suffering, erring, and the downtrodden. Then the heart is free from pride and able to see God.

"Blessed are the peacemakers." These not only make peace but are not at peace unless they bring others into peace.

"Blessed are the persecuted." Persecution is the wage of those that keep the Beatitudes. For a thousand years no people has been so despised as have we and this is the sign that we have the truth.

The Parables of Salt and Light

"Ye are the salt of the earth."

By the word "salt" he indicates what your office should be, for salt is not for itself and cannot salt itself, but it is to be used on meat and food in the kitchen, that they keep their taste fresh and not spoil. So says the Lord, "You are salt." Not the kind in the kitchen, of course, but the kind that salts the meat which is the whole world. This is a lordly office and a mighty honor that God calls you his salt and lays it upon you to salt the whole earth. But for this he needs a man ready to be poor, miserable, needy, gentle, and willing to suffer persecution, shame, and reviling. Without all this the preacher is savorless salt. To be a preacher is hard, and flesh and blood are not equal to it; but there must be those who do it gladly, since God and the Lord Jesus do not compel or drive us here with commandments. To be a Christian calls for a willing heart, and he who has no heart for it had better stay away. Our comfort is this, that when the world and the devil glower at us, Christ says to us, "You are the salt of the earth." But to salt the world is to offend the world. Salt stings. Some say that we should not reprove the pope and the bishops and the princes because this will cause resentment, but if you are going to preach the gospel and help people, you have to be sharp and rub salt into the wounds. One has to reprove what is not right such as Masses, monasticism, and indulgences that such offenses may be corrected. Christ speaks of the salt which has lost its savor and that means the salt which has lost its sting.

"Ye are the light of the world."

Christ here wishes to say: "If you will be my preachers, you must take your stand before the world as on a high mountain. You must be of good courage and openly proclaim without reserve.... You are neither to hold your peace nor to speak out of respect for anyone. Since you are a light, you are to shine without regard to honor or shame, riches or poverty, hate or favor, death or life. Remember that you are serving me, for it is I who have set you for a light."

"Let your light so shine before men, that they may see your good works."

Matthew, Mark, and Luke are inferior to John on this point. They harp on good works because good works are to be forgotten.

The Law

"Think not that I am come to destroy the law or the prophets."

Formerly we used expressions now used by the Antinomians [who reject all the works of the law], but things are different now. It was necessary then to emphasize forgiveness because at that time we were more than sufficiently crushed and trembled at the falling of a leaf. Not only Olympus but even heaven and hell quaked before the pope or any paltry priest. I recall how I myself broke out with sweat and even to this day I cannot look joyfully as I ought on my Lord Jesus because of that pestilential picture of him as judge. But these Antinomians now take the sermons intended at that time for the crushed and address them instead to the complacent.

"Thou shalt not kill; . . . but I say, . . . Whosoever is angry."

In this passage, there are four grades of anger. The first is the most important. It is the anger of the heart because the heart must be transformed into friendliness if you would be a Christian and that will never take place completely in life. The second form of anger is that which breaks out so that a man is ugly, and the third is when one says, "you fool." All railing is forbidden. The fourth is when the hand is stretched out to kill rather than to help. If I do not help, I am guilty of killing. By that token I think all rich men are murderers and all clerics are homicides.

The law says you must be pure, but who is? Human nature will not confer purity. It comes from heaven. Sometimes I refrain from sin because I fear the penalty—punishment, disgrace, and hell. Although I may appear friendly, I am like Cain with a false heart toward my brother. I talk with him civilly, but inside I am saying, "May lightning strike you." Look at what Christ enjoins, and you will see that you do not keep a word of it. The heart is full of bitterness. If I say, "I will not get angry," it's no use. One can scarcely hold back for half an hour, just as one cannot stop fire from burning.

"Thou shalt not commit adultery."

The third grade of adultery is to look upon a woman to desire her. Is that not the hardest of all Christ's commands? Girls lead the boys on by drooping their eyelids and by not wearing hats over their eyes. The modest maid Rebecca when she saw Isaac, her bridegroom, coming toward her, put a veil over her face. Saint Elizabeth was reproved because she gave loving glances to her husband in church. What, then, shall we say to those who come to church to ogle and to be ogled?

"Swear not."

This means that no one should swear at his own inclination, but if it will help his neighbor, he may do so.

"Turn the other cheek."

The way of peace is not when each demands his own and will suffer no wrong. If there is to be peace, someone has to give way to the other and suffer. If one does contend and strive, in the end after untold damage is done, this has to stop. God had ordained that he who will not let a little go in obedience to his command will lose much or all through feuds and wars. He who for the love of an eternal reward will not forgive his neighbor six or ten gulden will be compelled for the devil's sake to give to the judge twenty or thirty or forty. Big lords make wars over peccadilloes and for the sake of a trifling right involve a land in incalculable loss. This is the perverted wisdom of the world that fishes with a golden net, and the cost is greater than the profit.

Almsgiving

"When thou doest thine alms, do not sound a trumpet before thee."

Many [says Luther] give for the sake of recognition. If this were not the motive, they would not be repelled by ingratitude, but would say, "I did not do this for my sake, nor for my sake will I stop, but I will go

Beginnings of the Ministry

on for God's honor and pleasure even though no one give me a good word for it." You grumble and say: "I have done so much for this fellow; but he soon forgets, and I have no thanks. I would gladly have plucked the heart out of my body for him, but when he shows no thankfulness I would rather go to hell than spend another copper or give him another crust of bread." See [says Luther] the knave peering through your mask. Your very words prove that you have done this in order that people may make a fuss over you and treat you as a god.

The Lord's Prayer

"Our Father."

God desires that you lay before him all your need, not because he does not know but that your heart may be kindled and desire more and that you may spread your apron to receive it.

"Hallowed be thy name."

This is not German. We should say, "Heavenly Father, may thy name be holy." But what does that mean? It is not already holy? Of course, but in our usage it must be holy. Since in this prayer we call God "father," we should be devoted children. We should not abuse his name by swearing, cursing, lying, and deception.

"Thy kingdom come."

God's Kingdom is nothing other than that we should be godly, disciplined, pure, mild, gentle, kindhearted, full of all virtue and grace, and that he alone may live and reign in us. When these virtues are present, then without any effort on our part, joy, peace, blessedness, and all delight will follow.

"Thy will be done."

You say, "But has not God given us a free will?" To be sure, he has. But are you to make it into your will so that he will no longer be free? If you do with him as you will, then he is not free, but he is yours. In this prayer God teaches us to pray against ourselves, for we have no greater enemy than ourselves. Our will is the greatest thing we have, and yet against this will we must pray: "O Father, let me not seek to have my way, break my will, avert my will. Let come to me what may, that it may be according to thy will, not mine. As it is in heaven where no one has his own way, so may it be on earth." If such a prayer is heard, it hurts nature because this is nothing other than to pray for the cross, martyrdom, suffering, and the destruction of our will.

"Give us this day our daily bread."

When you pray this prayer you are not to think just of a flour bin and a baking oven but of wide land and all of God's provision. This covers all the blessings of this life, including peace and security. This is why rulers should emblazon on their shields not a lion nor place on their heads a jeweled crown, or stamp figures on their coins, but for an emblem on all they should use a loaf of bread, that subjects should recognize how through their office we enjoy that protection and peace without which we should have no bread.

This petition, though so brief, has the widest extent and could readily be expanded into a long prayer with all particulars, for example: "May

God give us to eat and drink, may he provide clothes, shelter, a sound body, make grain to grow and fruit to ripen, give us ordered households, godly wives and children. May he bless the work of our hands, give us faithful neighbors and friends, and grant to the kaiser and king and particularly to our princes power and favor that they may rule and rout the Turks. Bestow upon all subjects obedience, peace, and harmony among themselves. Deliver us from all perils of the body, from storm, hail, fire, and water, poison, pestilence, death of cattle, war, and bloodshed, hard times, wild animals, and bad men."

"When Ye Fast" (Matt. 6:16)

Christ said that we are not to engage in conspicuous fasts, but we have instituted first fourteen and then forty days, not to mention special days. All of them are not worth a heller. What kind of fast is it to dine on savory fish? As a matter of fact there may be prisoners and poor folk who fast from necessity, but I don't know any who fast for piety. There is less and less fasting. My dear papists are all turning into good Lutherans, but they let our poor preachers go hungry and do the fasting for them. The distinction of foods is ridiculous—to prohibit fowl and allow fish with strong wine. But I would approve of a fast ordered by the government of refraining from meat two days a week to save food, and once a week I think it would be well to go to bed on only bread and drink, but this is a matter of civil administration. And I think fasts on special occasions and on every Friday would be wholesome as signs of religious events, but I would not institute these fasts. The real fast is to keep your body under discipline in food, drink, sleep, and everything else. Such a fast is not kept, not even by the Carthusians.

"Lay Not up for Yourselves Treasures upon Earth" (Matt. 6:19)

Does this mean not to lay up anything at all? Oh, no! For God put silver and gold in mines, and Joseph laid by for the seven lean years. Christ is here talking to a man as a Christian, not as a citizen, because a Christian is neither man nor wife, young nor old, lord nor servant, emperor, prince, peasant nor townsman, nor anything else in the world because his treasure is in heaven. A prince can be a Christian, but he does not rule as a Christian. As to his person he is a Christian, but his office as a prince has nothing to do with Christianity. In his role as a Christian the gospel teaches him to wrong no one, punish no one, love everyone, and to suffer injury. This is a lesson for Christians, but if that were said to a prince, he could not carry on his administration. A prince must say: "My status as a Christian is between God and me, but in the world I have another status or office. This role is not between me and God but between me and my land and my people. It is not a question here of what I should suffer. That applies to my person as a Christian, but as a prince I must administer justice, maintain the peace, punish the bad, and protect the good." You see these estates or offices are distinguished and yet united in the same person and yet stand over against each other. The same person should both suffer and not suffer according to his office. In my role as a Christian I suffer, but in my capacity as a civil person, bound to .land and people whom I must help and protect and for whose sake the sword has been placed in my hand, I am not to suffer but the contrary. So each man on earth has in himself two persons, one for himself bound only to God and the other in a civil role in which he is bound to other people.

So also with regard to this text. As a Christian I am not to lay up treasures, but every town should save for emergencies and the churches should have common chests for the poor. However, the heart should not be avaricious.

On Anxiety

"Take no thought for your life."

For the greater part of the year man trusts in God. When the field is sown, it is left to God, but when the grain is reaped and in a barn man starts to worry about it. We sleep half our lives and who looks after us then? In fact, man does leave to God all except perhaps one tenth or one twentieth of his life. So why then is he everlastingly worried about the rest of it? If he is going to worry all the time, might he not better be dead? Observe how quickly danger passes, anxiety ceases, and man is happy again. Why? Because the danger is passed? In part, but not entirely. He is happy because he has stopped worrying about himself, for our worry brings a cross, but God's care brings peace and quiet.

"Behold the fowls of the air."

God is not talking about birds in cages. He looks after the birds better out of doors. See how fat and healthy they are! What beautiful vests and trousers they have! They are more beautiful than any haberdasher can make them because God is their weaver and tailor. If I look at the birds, they make me blush. A bird can say to me: "Christ preached about me in Matt., ch. 5, and made me into his doctor. See how fat and fine I am. If you want to know where my food is found, I'll tell you. The Heavenly Father is my farmer, servant, thresher, and reaper." That's the way a bird preaches the gospel to me. Again he may say: "See what a farmer works for me and how plump I am. Wherever I fly there is my cellar and if all the merchants, smiths, and carpenters came together, they could not make such a cellar and home. You too have big cellars, but what are they compared with mine? I sing before I eat. I am not anxious, because my kitchen and cellar are so big that I cannot fly beyond them. What is your cellar compared to that? See how shameful it is when you do not wait upon God." Ought we not to be ashamed of ourselves when the bird sings? If the bird could speak, he would say to us: "You have to have an annual market at Frankfurt to get your clothes. Because you don't trust in the Heavenly Father, you have to have money." "They sow not, neither do they reap." They do not take a single stalk home with them. How could Christ more severely reprimand us than by pointing to the birds?

"Judge Not" (Luke 6:37)

Everyone does. The wiser and more religious a person is the more he judges. If he discovers another in sin, he chortles. The heart has no mercy unless there be faith in Christ. Otherwise it is full of censure, and the respectable and gifted are the worst. The most honorable women have a serpent's tongue. They say, "Look at this one; look at that one." But the Christian knows that one is as good as another and that Saint Paul is no better than the thief on the cross nor an honorable maiden better than Mary Magdalene. Of course, on earth one is better than another, but do not flaunt your virtue in the name of the gospel, for this only makes you worse.

Your mercy should not be like that of scoundrels. Mercenary soldiers are murderers and rascals, but they are merciful to one another. You must be merciful, as is your Father in heaven. Behold how God gives corn, oats, milk, butter, and cheese like waves, so that the whole earth has enough to do gathering them in. He sends wagonsful into the Joachimstal and fills whole mountains with silver. He does not cover his sun with a napkin but lets it shine on thieves, murderers, and peasants. Nor does he stop because men are ungrateful.

The Narrow Gate (Matt. 7:13–14)

Christ wishes to warn his own that each must live in the world as if he were alone. When I see my neighbor, my city, and the whole world doing otherwise, when I see all the great, noble, and rich princes and lords going the way of the world, then I have a comrade greater than they, namely, Christ and his Word. Therefore when I walk alone I am not alone because I have Christ beside me and all the angels and saints from the beginning of the world. There is about me a greater crowd and a more lordly procession. With my eyes I note that many people fall away from me and are against me. If one walks according to the sight of the eyes, the offense will be crushing, for this is the strongest argument of the Turks, "Do you think God is so cruel that he will condemn such a large world?" And the papists say the same thing: "Do you think that what you have hatched in your little corner can alone be right and condemn all the rest of the world? Can so many popes, bishops, holy fathers, kings, and princes have all been mistaken?" They are absolutely sure on this account that our teaching cannot be right, but the only reason they offer is: "We are many; they are few. We are godly, learned, wise, God's people. We sit in the seats of the apostles. It is not possible that God should condemn so many excellent people for the sake of so few, since he did not make heaven for nothing."

"Narrow is the way, . . . and few there be that find it."

But Christ tells us to abide by God's Word. What was the Virgin Mary to do when the angel came to her and brought her the news that she was to be the mother of the Most High? Who stood at her side to believe this with her? And how was Abraham, when he went out from Ur of the Chaldees, to know that he alone was a Christian and all the world condemned?

In a word, our flesh wants to take the broad way and when we take the narrow the world persecutes us, hangs, burns, kills, and drowns, and the devil plagues our hearts with evil thoughts, doubts, fears, anxiety, desperation, and makes all our good into sin and shame. But Christ tells us to direct our feet toward the narrow gate, and he will make the way smooth for us and even dear and sweet.

4

The Miracles and the Parables

The Cure of the Deaf and Dumb (Mark 1:31–37)

The miracle of the cure of the deaf-and-dumb man is insignificant compared to what God does every day. For every day children are born who previously had neither ears nor tongues, nor indeed even a soul. In less than a year they are furnished with soul, body, tongue, and everything else. But this miracle is so common that no one pays any attention to it. Scarcely anyone in the world ever says thank you to God for his tongue and his ears. How many are there who having enjoyed good sight for fifty years ever give God thanks with all their hearts? How many rejoice over so great a miracle? They marvel that Christ healed this man, but not that they themselves are able to hear. By this little miracle God stirs us up to .recognize the great miracles. The whole world is deaf not to hear this. Pythagoras was considered a heretic because he heard the wonderful song of the stars. But one who is not blind will see the heavens so wondrous that one could die for very joy over the sight. If we had eyes and ears, we would be able to see and hear what the wheat says to us: "Rejoice in God, eat and drink, use me and serve your neighbor. Soon I will fill the barns." If I were not deaf, I would hear what the cows say: "Be glad, we bring butter and cheese. Eat and drink and give to others." So the hens say, "We lay eggs for you." And the birds,

"Be joyful, we are hatching chicks." And the sows grunt for joy because they bring pork and sausages. So speak all the animals to us, and everyone should say, "I will use what God has given, and I will give to others."

But as Christ effected this cure he sighed because he knew that as soon as the man's tongue was restored he would misuse it.

The Widow's Son (Luke 7:11–17)

The widow would not have so appreciated God's work if she had not first been in anguish. So it is in life. If God did not let the sun rise for two days, what an outcry there would be! In order that we may appreciate his benefits, he suffers us first to be deprived of everything.

This woman saw only that her son was dead. No one discovered any sign that he would ever speak again. Therefore faith resides in those things which neither reason nor flesh nor feeling can see. Someday we shall feel, but now the old Adam is so blind that when he is in penury he does not see how he can be helped, nor when in torment of conscience how he can be comforted. So this widow saw not that Christ was the one who would help her. That is why Paul says that God does for us more than we can ask or think. (Eph. 3:20.) And again, "The Spirit helps our infirmities: for we know not for what we should pray." (Rom. 8:26.) When a man truly prays, there is something higher in him, so that he does not know how much he should ask nor how much God will give him. This woman was so dejected that she longed indeed to have her son back but did not dare ask it because her doubt was mightier. Thus we see how deeply God peers into our hearts.

Christ perceives the longing and does not ask about the words in the mouth. He hears only the cry of the heart, and such a cry breaks through the heavens and the clouds and will be heard. God does not look at what we ask. We ask for some little thing, and he says: "That is far too small. I'll give you something else that is far greater than you yourself." So in doubt and death he gives me greater things than I know and see. Then I say, "Yes, I wanted it, but I did not know I should ask for it." This woman saw only her heart's sorrow. Then God gave her more and deeper things than she understood.

That her son was dead was plain, and the life in which she must believe was nothing and yet must be something. Such must be the thoughts and the faith of every Christian in all things that touch life. He must say, "I know that it is, although I see nothing." This is a great art in which I am only a pupil.

Our whole life is comprised in this same word. We have indeed Christ; we have eternal life, eternal justification, health, and comfort, and where are they? We see them not; they are not in a drawer, in the hands, but just in the Word. So God encompasses his doing in nothing. That is why you cannot tell a Christian by looking at him, because he can be recognized only by his speech, for Christ himself said, a Christian is like the wind. One hears the sound thereof, "but whence it comes and whither it goes, one knows not." If one touches with the hand, it is not there. So is it with the Christian. I cannot recognize him because he is learned, rich, or wise, but only when through the rushing of the wind I perceive that he has the Word. He who would be a genuine Christian must be able to say that he has and believes in God, who can count out money from a naked purse and pour a drink from an empty cup.

So it was at the recent Reichstag. There were two gods there, God and the devil with all his wiles. But the Word stood, and we with the Word, and that's enough and more than ten Turkish kaisers. The lack is only in us to fathom the grace we have been given. Let us hold fast to this—that it is God's Word for which we fought and put ourselves in danger. Our opponents had to confess that our teaching is right and good.

Let us then rise toward God and desire those things which are not, as this mother had no son but would have him out of nothing. So when I die, I go into nothingness. I see nothing. I feel nothing. Then first God is known and herein I know what he is, namely, he that makes something to be out of nothing. About me is darkness. He says, "Let there be light and life," and out of nothing it is so. Thus from death I am made to be life.

The Miracle of the Loaves and Fishes
(Mark 6:30–44)

Reason says that loaves cannot be multiplied. It is something great when a man believes what he does not see. If one believes in Christ, the impossible becomes the possible. It is so when we

are in danger of death, and the Christian says, "It is impossible that I should remain alive, but I believe." He breaks through the impossible and says it is possible. Similarly when a man feels the sting of sin, reason says: "You are lost. You have sinned. Who can make sin to be not sin?" But a Christian goes farther and says, "Although sin is here and no one can make sin to be not sin, nevertheless I will break through and claim that there is no sin in me." The Christian is a giant who puts through impossibilities. But where are such people?

Yet in the last five or six years [prior to 1528] our cause has gone farther than reason would have believed. It seemed impossible that we should be so long in peace. Our enemies are too many to count—the rabble, the princes, the bishops. If anybody had told the emperor and kings six years ago that today we would still be preaching, they would have bet their crowns against it. So it is in all things. A Christian must do the impossible, make a just man out of a sinner, devour death, and swallow the devil.

[But to get back to the loaves.] Christ tells us to pray for our daily bread. He gives greater honor to bread than to gold or silver. Bread, not gold, rejoices the heart of man. Reason says, "If I have gold, I'll have enough to eat"; but Christ takes the meanest thing and gives it honor, "How many loaves have you?" he asks. They said, "Five loaves and two fishes." Now fish is the lowest form of meat. See how he glorifies bread with a miracle and fish too, as if he would say: "You should not scramble after goods and gold. How would it help you to have a whole temple full of Hungarian gulden?" If you had no bread, you would give all the money for a single slice. If you have nothing to eat, don't blame bread, but your own lack of faith. He who believes will have enough. Christ is the best baker. Believe on him, and you will have a baker who before you ask him starts baking bread.

And remember that farmers, millers, and bakers are the fingers of Christ.

In the last six years, I have seen many a man suffering from hunger who in the end was fed.

The guilds are so worried lest they have not enough to eat that they will not admit to membership a man of illegitimate birth. But is the man to blame that he was born out of wedlock? Is that any reason that he should not be a shoemaker? Must he expiate the sins of his father? Is he not as much created as you? Does he not have the same God and Father as you? "Brother" you should call him and he you because he is baptized. You say that your practice is the custom of the country, but God lets grain grow for the man whom you despise quite as much as for you. Suppose there should be more people at work, the work could be better done. One should not ask how many people there are. Just see how many there are in this town, and yet all have enough. Even if it were the custom of one hundred thousand cities to behave as you do, it would not be right.

[From another sermon on the same theme.] Christ can increase the bread in the house when you do not know how it happens. I notice it. I know that I spend more than I have. It is the same with a day laborer. He has children, and he does not see how he will be able to pay the rent. How does he manage it? The Lord once more works this miracle. Constantly he feeds us. This is nothing compared to the miracle which the farmer sees before his eyes. He works over his field and throws out a handful of seed and then a sprout comes up and bears ears full of grain. Out of the sand, wheat grows. [*Wittenberg* means the white hillock, so named because built on a mound of sand.] This is as much a miracle as making grain grow from a rock.

The whole land and the whole world are full of such miracles, but because the occurrence is daily and all men enjoy bread no one pays any attention. The miracle of the multiplication of the five loaves was really nothing compared to making bread out of stony ground, because making loaves out of a loaf already made of barley is not as much as to get bread from rocks. The seed has to lose its being and become a different creature by bringing from the earth a stalk for our comfort that we may see how good God is to us. But all this does not help because it is too common.

Look at your body. In three hours, bread is converted into flesh and blood. Do you think the heat of your stomach does it? There is a great deal more heat in an oven than in you. What then turns bread into flesh and blood? Nothing other than the Word of God. See then that bread comes not from the field but from the hand of the Lord. Even if there were no bread, we should not die of hunger, because the body is sustained by the Word. . . . God has also given us cows and sheep for milk and wool.

The Cure of the Nobleman's Son (John 4:46–54)

The nobleman might have hesitated to approach Christ. He might have said: "He won't hear me. He will snub me." Had he taken this attitude he would have been lost, but because he put behind him such thoughts Christ said, "Thy son liveth." Such is the nature of faith. That was what Paul had in mind when he said, "We reflect

with unveiled face the glory of the Lord and are transformed from glory into glory" (II Cor. 3:18). When we recognize Christ as the one who helps, who gives power to fulfill the law and through whom we have the forgiveness of sins, then as the sun is reflected from water or a mirror, so Christ is reflected from the heart, and we are transformed from glory into glory. Daily we increase and know the Lord better, for we are changed into the same image and are baked together with Christ into one loaf.

"Sir, come down ere my child die."

Such is the human heart. It thinks, "He will certainly die." The nobleman can think of nothing but this: "My son is dying." But the moment he hears the words, "Thy son liveth," he is completely changed. The same heart which is sure he would die is sure he is alive. This is what John means by believing in the Word. Absolutely nothing was seen or felt. Where do we find such Christians? Truly they are a pure miracle. Yet, we must come to such faith or go under. We must hold only to the Word even though we see no sign.

Peter's Failure to Walk on the Water (Matt. 14:22–36)

Peter cried, "Lord, help me," and Christ did not fail him but helped him on the instant. It was high time; otherwise Peter would have gone fishing at the bottom of the lake and would never have brought in any more fish to the market at Bethesda. But Christ was his helper in need.

Then Christ chided Peter that he was so unbelieving and full of doubt. Christ laid the blame squarely on Peter and not on the sea or the wind. Christ did not say: "You sea, and you storm, why have you done this? Why did you want to drown my apostle?" But he said: "Peter, why had you so little faith? The sea is not to blame. It did only that which is its nature to do, and you had to take what it is your nature to take. If you had been brave and risen above your nature, the sea also would have given up its nature. You could have gone on farther, and the sea would still have been to you as earth and a strong rock." Doubt and faith make all the difference. Faith makes the sea into a dry way and doubt for Peter turns a dry way into a sea.

The Canaanite Woman (Matt. 15:21–28)

The woman said, "Lord, help me," and if he didn't give her a death blow when he told her to her face she was a dog and not worthy to share the children's bread! What could she say to that? He told her she was one of the damned and lost and could not be counted among the elect. That was a final irrevocable answer, and nobody could get away from it. But she did not give up. She agreed with him that she was a dog and asked no more than a dog, that she should eat the crumbs that fell from the master's table. Was that not tremendous! She caught Christ in his own words. What could he do now? He opened his heart and answered her wish and made her not a dog, but a child of Israel.

This is written for our comfort and instruction that we may know how deeply God hides his grace from us and that we must not think

of him according to our ideas and feeling, but only according to his Word. Here we see that though Christ speaks harshly he does not give a final judgment, an absolute "no." All his answers sound like "no," but are not exactly, but hang in the air. He did not say she was not of the house of Israel but only that he was not sent save to the house of Israel. His answer wavered between "yes" and "no." He did not say she was a dog but only that it is not proper to take the children's food and give it to the dogs. Again he left it hanging whether or no she was a dog. The "no" sounds stronger than the "yes," but nevertheless there was more there of "yes" than of "no," a pure "yes," deep and secret.

This shows the state of our heart when sore pressed. Christ in this story behaves the way the heart feels, for it thinks the answer is "no" when in reality it is not. Therefore the heart must turn away from its feeling and lay hold of the deep, secret "yes" under the "no," with firm faith in God's Word, as did this woman.

The Parable of the Sower (Mark 4:3–8)

"And brought forth, some thirty, and some sixty, and some a hundred." This has been interpreted to mean that virginity rates one hundredfold, widowhood sixty, and marriage only thirty. This

is altogether too narrow an interpretation. Paul enumerates many more fruits of the spirit than chastity (Gal. 5:22). Besides, widowhood, marriage, and virginity are not fruits or good works, rather they are estates ordained by God, and they do not lie within our power. I will say further that chastity is higher than virginity. A virgin according to her nature is a woman capable of childbearing. She feels attraction for a man, but chastity is absence of desire and that is why there is more chastity in marriage because there is less desire. Virginity can even be less chaste than marriage. What this parable does mean is that in some localities one hundred are converted; in some, sixty; and in some, thirty.

The Parable of the Tares (Matt. 13:24–30)

In the previous parable the seed was the Word of God and the field the heart of man, but in this parable the field is the world. The wheat means the good children and the tares the bad. Here the Gospel teaches us that we are not to expect the true Christian faith and the pure word of God to prevail in the world. There must be false teachers and heretics. We are not to be affrighted by this because the devil is always among the children of God. As for the treatment of these heretics we are here told that we are not to exterminate them, since he who errs today may turn to the right course tomorrow. Who knows if the word of God will touch his heart? But if he is burned or strangled, he is prevented from coming to the truth and thus he is lost who might have been saved. The Lord points out furthermore the danger that the wheat will be destroyed along with the tares. See, then, how frightful we have been that for so long we have handled the Turks with the sword, heretics with fire, and have sought by killing to force the Jews to the faith, to root out the tares by our own power, as if we were the people to rule over hearts and spirits.

I would rather tolerate an entire unchristian land for the sake of one Christian in the midst than to exterminate one Christian with the unchristians. The papists then turn this statement against us and say that we ought not to have suppressed the Mass and the cloisters at Wittenberg. But they misread the text. The Lord does not say that we should not avoid but only that we should not exterminate. But if they insist that we should allow the Mass and the cloisters to grow until the harvest, thereby they confess that they are tares.

Nor is the church itself ever wholly pure. Noah thought that he had a pure church in the ark, but then his son Ham rose up and mocked him. When God builds a church the devil always constructs a chapel alongside.

[Luther insists that we are not to understand the tares as sins which are to be allowed to grow until the harvest.]

You are not to say, "Since my sins are taken away, I will sin without a care, because sins cannot damn me any more." No, you should say: "Dear Lord, thou hast forgiven me; thou hast forgiven my sins out of sheer grace. Help me henceforth to delight in thy Word and Sacrament, to praise and honor thy Son with thankfulness that thy name may be hallowed by me, thy Kingdom come to me, thy will be done in me, that I may grow into a joyous person, who with liking and love does and suffers as the holy martyrs did, who took no thought of death, devil, and hell. . . ."

We Christians understand that in our body there are still corruption, sin, and impurity. Nevertheless, God treats us as pure because we have begun to believe in Christ and because we shall go on to believe more; and we shall always be amazed and say: "Heavenly Father, is it so? Shall I believe that thou hast sent thy Son into the world and hast given him to me, and that for me he had to become a man and shed his blood?" Indeed, yes, and there is no doubt that I must further say, "Truly, every day of my life I will thank God for it, praise him and glorify him and never again steal, take usury, covet, or be proud and envious."

The Good Samaritan (Luke 10:30–37)

The good Samaritan is a type of Christ who takes the half-dead sinner to his hospital. Is the sick man then just? No, he is a sinner, yet at the same time just. A sinner in fact, but just because God has regard to him and has given a sure promise that he will make him free and at last will completely heal him of his sin. Thus in hope he is perfectly well, though in reality he is a sinner. But he has made a beginning toward righteousness and will progress toward it, though he always recognizes himself as unrighteous.

So also in the church we are healed, though not altogether as yet. On account of the one we are called "flesh," on account of the

other "spirit." It is the whole man who loves purity, and it is the whole man who is sunk in desire. There are two whole men and yet only one whole man. That is why man fights with himself and is his own enemy. He will and at the same time he will not. But precisely here is the glory of the grace of God that it makes us into enemies of ourselves.

The Great Banquet (Luke 14:15–24)

[There was a man who gave a great feast and invited many, but they began to make excuse. Then he sent his servants and compelled them to come in.] They began to make excuse. "The gospel," they would say, "is a teaching which will not let us do as we please. It demands body and life, gold and goods to be risked for Christ's sake. Therefore we will not come. We are going to keep our houses safe." They want to keep their cattle, land, wife, and child all secure, so they fill cellar and kitchen and think they are godly and that God has blessed them. So our Papists say that our teaching is true enough but that one must stay with the church. Or they say that our teaching is revolutionary and will overthrow the government. They have the same fear as the Jews in Jesus' day that they will lose their church and their government.

Then the host was angry and told his servants to go into the highways and byways and compel them to come in. That is what will happen to our assailants, and it will not help them that they are bishops and mighty princes and suppose that the Lord will not reject them on that account or accept that little rat's nest of a Wittenberg. Yes, my dear friend, if he rejected the best among his chosen people, he will not spare you because you are so holy and mighty. You need not think that you will eat bread in heaven because it is to the poor that the gospel is preached.

What does he mean by "compel them to come in"? Does God desire forced service? It means that they must be so crushed through fear of the wrath of God as to be ready to receive help. When the heart is smitten and affrighted, then comes the further word, "Dear man, do not despair even if you are a sinner and under such judgment."

Be baptized, hear the gospel, and you will hear that Jesus Christ has died for you and taken away your sin.

The Lost Sheep (Luke 15:3–7)

Dear friends, since I have nothing else to preach about I will take the gospel for the day. We are the lost sheep. Christ takes the lamb on his shoulders. This means that we are not to rely on ourselves but trust wholly to him. But one must make a distinction. To the hard of heart, the bad sheep, one preaches condemnation, but to the lost sheep, consolation. To the thresher in the harvest give cheese, bread, and thin beer; but to another, something sweet. Spare me the law until I am obstinate, then I will eat onions with Sodom and go under the Red Sea like Pharaoh. The lost sheep are those who are fearful and troubled, and they need a different dish from the bad sheep. When the heart quakes and crumbles and despairs because God is not gracious, there is a sheep that can believe (Ps. 119:176): "I am a lost and straying sheep. Seek thou thy servant." It is not the obstinate who talk that way but the anxious. Give them sugar that the heart may be quickened, lest they fall into despair. They are to be set upon their feet, not through Moses but through Christ: "Because you are a lost sheep, I will wrap you in a blanket and put you in a wagon or carry you about my neck."

The Prodigal Son (Luke 15:11–32)

The prodigal's return began not with the fear of punishment, but his repentance came from this, that his father inwardly drew him and love for his father's house flowed through him, for he said: "How many hired servants are in my father's house?. . .1 am not worthy to be called thy son." Such a sigh God sees and hears. The prodigal said this in words, but more important were the anguish and the crushing of his heart. This came before the groaning in his throat and the upward sigh. In this music, to us the most painful and doleful, God has more joy than in any other service of worship, as

Isaiah said (ch. 57:15), "I will dwell with those who are of a broken and contrite spirit."

The Rich Man and Lazarus (Luke 16:19–31)

The rich man was an honorable man, but the Gospel has sharp eyes and sees deeply into the bottom of the heart and reproves works that reason cannot reprove. The rich man was not condemned because he wore costly raiment—so did Solomon, Esther, David, Daniel, and others—but that he made of this an idol. The secret sin of his heart was lack of faith, for he who is without faith makes of his belly a god and neglects his neighbor. But through faith man sees how good and gracious is God and through this knowledge his heart is made tender and merciful, so that he would gladly do to every man what God has done to him. Therefore he breaks out with love and serves his neighbor with his whole heart, with body and life, with goods and honor, with soul and spirit, and stakes all for the neighbor, as God has done for him.

Likewise suffering and poverty do not make one acceptable to God, but if one is first acceptable, then suffering and poverty are precious in his sight.

Tell me, what king with all his wealth has ever done the world so much good as this Lazarus with his sores? With what masterly stroke God puts to shame that clever fool reason and wordly wisdom! She prefers to look at the purple of the rich man and holds her nose at the wounds of Lazarus and averts her eyes from his loathsomeness. God lets the great fool pass over the costly treasure, speaks his judgment in the stillness, and makes the poor man so dear and precious that all the kings are not worthy to wash his sores. So today we destroy the saints and then out of their clothes, shoes, and vessels we make holy relics, institute pilgrimages, build churches on their graves, and with such nonsense make fools of ourselves.

The Grateful Samaritan (Luke 17:11–19)

[Out of ten lepers cured only one returned to give thanks, and he a Samaritan.]

God desires only to be loved and lauded by us. Therefore the psalm says: "What will you give me? Is not all mine? Sacrifice to me the sacrifice of praise." (Ps. 50:12–14, paraphrased.)

So now he will say to those who endow incense, choirs, bell ringers, and candles: "Do you suppose I am blind or deaf or that I have no dwelling place? You should love and praise me. Instead you smoke and clang bells."

First we must taste and see how sweet the Lord is. (Ps. 34:8; I Peter 2:3.) This experience comes to faith at the end of the trial, for during strife and tribulation faith is at work, and though when it is bitter and hard, yet when the evil hour is over, if we but hold on and stand firm, then comes the sweetness of God.

The Pharisee and the Publican (Luke 18:9–14)

The publican beat his breast. Faith is so active that it has to express itself. Christ said he was justified, but it was not because he beat his breast. What was wrong with the Pharisee? This, that he did not know his own sin. See, God's sword cuts to the nerve of the soul. As the Pharisee starts to pray, "God, I thank thee," God breaks in, "Yes, yes, yes, I hear well enough that you have no need of God, that you despise his goodness and mercy and all that he is." And that is why public sins like adultery and murder are not to be compared with this sin of unbelief which lies in the heart and which we do not see. This is the real sin.

5

The Journey to Jerusalem and Holy Week

Fire from Heaven (Luke 9:51–56)

"Lord, wilt thou that we command fire to come down from heaven, and consume them?" asked the disciples. Oh, you disciples! You think that anyone who does not accept Jesus is going straight to hell, and if he won't give Jesus lodging, you say, "To the devil with you." Observe from this passage that the Holy Spirit has a hard time to cool the intemperate zeal of the godly. Christ said, "Just remember whose children you are, namely, children of the Holy Spirit, a spirit of peace and not dissension." Peter in the Garden forgot that and Christ told him to put up his sword into the scabbard, because this was not the time to fight but to suffer. The Holy Spirit was silent when Christ was reviled and crucified. We are to be of a meek spirit, for the meek shall inherit the earth. This does not mean that we are to be silent when the truth is assailed. We do not fight the wicked because of their lives, but when they revile the word, we cannot be silent, but must speak. We are not, however, to be like James and John, wishing vengeance to descend upon the godless and the tyrants. In that case, we are murderers. If God can suffer them, why cannot we? Christ displayed enough zeal when he cried: "Woe unto thee, Chorazin!

woe unto thee, Bethsaida!" He tempered his tone when he added, "I praise thee, Father, Lord of heaven and earth, that thou hast hid these things from the wise and prudent, and revealed them unto babes." So also we should say: "Why should I be so hot? God will have it so." We are to take care not to put in our hand. God does not need our fighting. Here we are to suffer and leave vengeance to the Lord. Otherwise we have a bad spirit.

Peter's Confession (Matt. 16:13–17)

Observe that Christ did not address Peter alone, but all the apostles, since he said, "Who say ye that I am?" He did not say, "Peter, who do you say that I am?" Christ accepted Peter's answer as the answer of all the apostles and disciples. Otherwise he would have asked them one by one, and from this we may also infer that Christ did not say to Peter alone but to all the disciples: "Thou art Peter. . . . And I will give unto thee the keys of the kingdom of heaven." How would it be possible to state more clearly that Peter here is not Peter? For Christ said that he was not flesh and blood but the one to whom the Father in heaven had revealed this.

Peter, here, therefore, is not a person in his own right, but only a hearer of the Father making this disclosure. Not Simon Bar-Jona answers here, not flesh and blood, but the hearer of the Father's revelation.

Christ said that on this rock he would build his church. If we take this rock to be the power of the pope, what then follows? It will mean that the church of the apostles was no church at all, because for the span of eighteen years Peter was in Jerusalem and had not seen Rome. This can be clearly proved out of Paul's letter to the Galatians where he says that after his conversion he spent three years in Arabia and then went up to Jerusalem to see Peter, and again fourteen years after that he went up once more to Jerusalem to confer with James and John and Peter. Now, who could be so out of his mind as to say that there was at that time no church in Jerusalem because the power of the Roman Church was not yet established? The church is built not upon the rock taken to be the power of the Roman Church but on the faith that Peter confessed on behalf of the whole church. The universal, catholic church existed for so long prior to the Roman Church.

Peter and the Keys (Matt. 16:18–19)

Christ says here clearly that he gave the keys to Peter. He does not say two kinds of keys, but the keys which he gives to Peter, as if he would say: "Why do you scramble up to heaven after my keys? Haven't you heard that I left them on earth and gave them to Peter? You won't find them in heaven, but in Peter's mouth, where I left them. Peter's mouth is my mouth. His office is my office. His keys are my keys. I have no others; I know of no others. What they bind is bound; what they loose is loosed. If there are other keys in heaven or earth or in hell, I do not care about them, nor about what they bind or loose. You should not care about them either. Let them not lead you astray. Hold to Peter, that is, to *my* keys which bind and loose in heaven and no others." See, this is the proper way to think and speak about the keys. Any other interpretation is forced.

Peter and Tax Collecting (Matt. 17:24–27)

Christ came to Peter and said: "What do you think, Simon? From whom do the kings of the earth take toll or tribute? From their sons or from strangers?" Peter said, "From strangers." And Jesus said, "Therefore the children are free." This is a lovely story of Christ's attitude toward the government. First, he let Peter be asked by the tax gatherers for the yearly impost in order to have an opportunity to speak about the two kingdoms, the earthly and the heavenly. Before Peter could give an account, Christ came to him and asked from whom the kings of the earth take tribute. His meaning was: "I know very well, Peter, that we are kings and the sons of kings. I am myself the King of Kings. Therefore, no one has the right to take tribute from us. They should rather pay it to us. How is it then possible, my Peter, that they should levy a tax on you, since you are the son of a king? What do you think? Do they have a right to exact it from you?"

Since Christ put the question in a general way, Peter answered in all simplicity and in general, "Not the sons of the kings, but the strangers pay the tax." Peter did not perceive that by these words Christ meant to call him the son of a king. From this we see how genially Christ walked with his disciples. Here he joked and played with Peter as with a child. Because Peter was without guile, Christ took pleasure in his simplicity.

"Except Ye Become as Little Children" (Matt. 18:1–10)

When the disciples were disputing who would be the greatest in the Kingdom, Christ set in their midst a child barely able to toddle, thus to show that the greatest apostles, the pillars of Christendom, should learn from a child that could not speak and should say to him, "*Lieber Herr Doktor.*" When you see a child on his father's lap you should take off your hat and say, "Herr Doktor, we should be ashamed of ourselves before you." We must become as little children, because a child does not have in his heart the malice of a prince or a noble. He hears the Lord's Prayer and does not think of the things that disquiet our hearts. He wants to suck sugar in heaven and dreams with delight of golden apples. He leaves the big things to the bigwigs and rides on a hobbyhorse. When he hears of death he thinks of it as sleep. He grows in peace,

is fresh and sound. So also we must be young in Christ. If we were to become children, then the pope and I and all men would be of one heart and mind.

"Who is My Mother? and Who Are My Brethren?" (Matt. 12:48)

[Commenting on this text, Luther makes the point that we are not to obey anyone in disobedience to God.]

Our bishops, princes, and papists themselves confess, and must confess, that we have the word of God, and yet they say it is not valid unless commanded by them and confirmed by a council. But how now does the Christian church come to the point of striking God on the mouth and making him speechless? Saying:

"We confess that it is thy Word, but it is only to go into effect when we say so." What do you think God from his judgment seat will say to them? "My dear *Junker,* pope, bishops, and princes, whoever you may be, did you not know that it was my Word?" "Yes," you say. "Very well then, why did you not keep it? Because the Christian church did not command it? Are your churches then to control my word? I thought that when I opened my mouth, man would accept my word as settled; and that if all the world said the contrary, the world should be trodden under foot. How would you like it, if you gave a command to a servant in your house, and he went out and asked the maid or a fellow servant whether he should keep it?"

"Come unto Me" (Matt. 11:28)

By these words Christ means to say: "Come to me freely without any merit. You have no need to bring me fastings and other good works. Come only with the faith of the heart. Look upon me as a good and gracious Savior. There is no need for anything else. Simply come; I will quicken you. This is no make-believe. I will make your heart and your spirit bold against hell, sin, death, and devil. You will feel it. Now you have a bad conscience; you are depressed, crushed, miserable, poor, anxious, and worried, and there is no one who can give you counsel, comfort, and help. God's wrath against sin is so tremendous. Before his righteousness heaven and earth must bow and no one can be justified before him save through me. Come then to me. Confess your life to be pitiably bad. Such pupils are just the ones I want. This is the sort I invite. I have nothing to do with the well. My Kingdom is a hospital for the sick because I am a doctor. The right kind of patient in my hospital is the one who knows he is sick, who feels the pressure of sin, and who earnestly seeks from me health and comfort and believes that I shall help him. This is the one whom I will make joyful, and I will make him alive, that he shall nevermore die. Therefore, if anyone wishes health, a peaceful conscience, and a quiet heart, let him not run here and there, but come unto me."

Again Christ says, "Take my yoke upon you." That is why men

do not run to Christ. He puts a yoke on the old donkey. That means a cross. He lays a heavy burden on the neck. But Christ says: "Do not be downcast on this account. Take my yoke upon you; I will help you out of trouble. Let this be enough that I take from your soul the weight and the work and the bad conscience. Be patient if I flay the old ass. He must be killed if I am to make you alive. This is the nature of my Kingdom that those who would come in must constantly die to the desires of the old Adam and be renewed in the spirit through increase in faith."

"Where Two or Three Are Gathered Together" (Matt. 18:18–20)

When I am troubled and sad, distressed and discouraged, no matter what the time of day—for public preaching does not go on all the time in the churches—if then my neighbor or brother comes to me, I should unburden myself to him in the assurance that his word of comfort has God's "yes" in heaven. By the same token I am to comfort another and say: "Dear friend, dear brother, why not stop worrying? It is not God's will that sorrow should so afflict you. He has not sent his son to die for you that you should be downcast, but that you should be of good cheer; so then, be joyous and consoled. In that way you will do God a service and please him." Then we should kneel down and say the Lord's Prayer together. It will certainly be heard in heaven, for Christ said, "I am in your midst." He did not say, "1 see it; I hear it; and I shall come to you," but he said, "I am already there." When, then, you comfort me and I comfort you and both of us do it to our mutual improvement and blessing, then I should believe you and you should believe me that God, the Heavenly Father, will give us what we ask and what we lack.

Zacchaeus (Luke 19:1–10)

Zacchaeus did not want Christ to enter his house and yet he did. That he did not is plain because he climbed a tree to see Christ go by and did not dare to invite him because he did not consider himself to be worthy. He would be satisfied with a look and to

remain unrecognized. But that he really did want him to come is evident from this—that he received him with joy, for joy is the sign of a previous love and desire. If anyone had asked him whether he wanted Christ to come, he would have answered, "I do not dare to ask or to wish." Here one sees the depths of the human heart whose truth is so deep and whose desire is so hidden that it does not know itself nor rejoice in its own desire.

Jerusalem Beleaguered (Luke 21:20)

I am opposed to the fortification of Wittenberg. The advice that the Lord gave the disciples is best, "When you see Jerusalem compassed with armies . . . , flee." That is what they did. Whether we win or lose, we are done for. I will not be safe when unmarried soldiers have their way. When they come, we shall have to preach what they say or else they will give us nothing to eat. They will glut their lust with matron and maid. Kitchens and cellars must be opened to them. Even the princes will not fare any better. That is why I would not like to be here. I would rather await the end at the hands of the enemy, than so to be protected. Look at what happened in Vienna in peacetime from the soldiers there to defend the city against the Turks, and they behaved worse than the Turks. You cannot keep an army in a sack. That is why I am not in favor of the fortification and the garrisoning of Wittenberg. Christ told his disciples to flee, and that is what I say. If we knew the time of our visitation, we should have peace, but instead we drive out the preachers. Because we will not use the light of day, we shall see the night ablaze. And if the walls were as high as heaven and the iron as thick as church walls, still I would not stay because they will do no good. If Christ, the

Prince of Peace, is absent, even though the enemy without should do nothing, the city will be worse off within than on the outside.

Where will our souls be when all the world is consumed with fire? Tell me, my dear friend, where you are when you are asleep and do not know what is going on outside in the body? Do you think God is not able to hold the souls in his hand? Do you think he has to have a sheepfold for souls, like a shepherd? It is enough for you to know that souls are in the hands of God. Do not be disturbed because you do not understand how. The master said, "Father, into thy hands, I commend my spirit." Hold to that.

Mary and Martha (Luke 10:38–42)

Let us first take this as simply as it is told, for this is the greatest art—to abide by the simple understanding. The story is that Jesus came to a dwelling and although many people lived there, only Martha took him in. Now Martha had a sister. Mary. They divided the work. Martha went to prepare the food, carry the water, and wash the dishes. Now the Gospel says that this time Martha was doing all of this work alone. Christ had another work to do. He sat and preached and while Mary sat at his feet he took no heed of what Martha was doing. She came and complained, asking the Master to tell Mary to help her. "Look here," she said, "I have given myself so much trouble. I have been running around; I have washed up and put everything straight. Did I not have the right idea?" But God does not care about our idea. Jesus chided her not because of her work but because of her worry. "Martha, Martha," he said, "you are troubled about many things and only one thing is needful." As if he would say: "You are full of care and I have preached that we should have no care; and besides, when the Word is declared, other things should stop. Even more, we should forsake wife, child, father, mother, friends, and foe, honor, and goods, and cling only to the Word." You see, Martha had good intentions, yet he chided her; but he did it gently, and that is what is so fine about the Gospel. God is pictured as a kind, friendly man who deals tenderly with us when we do not do as we ought.

Palm Sunday (Matt. 21:1–9)

"Behold, thy King cometh unto thee, meek, and sitting upon an ass."

Look at Christ. He rides not upon a horse which is a steed of war. He comes not with appalling pomp and power but sits upon an ass, which is a gentle beast to bear burdens and to work for men. From this we see that Christ comes not to terrify, to drive, and oppress, but to help and to take for himself our load. We read further that he came from the Mountain of Olives. Now the oil of the olive was

the symbol of that which soothes. His entry was marked not by the clash of weapons and the cries of war, but by singing, praise, rejoicing, and the blessing of God.

"Thy King cometh unto thee."

Observe that he comes. You do not seek him; he seeks you. You do not find him; he finds you. The preachers come from him, not from you, and their preaching comes from him and not from you. Your faith comes, not from you, but from him.

He is lowly. This brings us from faith to the example of love. Christ gives you faith with all its benefits, and you are to give your neighbor love with all its benefits. You may then ask what are the good works which you should do for your neighbor? They have no name. Just as the good works which Christ has done for you have no name, so the good works which you do for your neighbor have no name. How, then, are they to be recognized? Answer: they have no name for this reason, lest they be divided and this done and that left undone. Rather you must give yourself to your neighbor utterly, just as Christ did not confine himself to prayer and fasting for you. These are not the works which he did for you, but he gave himself completely not only with prayer and fasting, with all works and suffering, so that there was nothing in him that was not made yours and done for you. So this is not your good work, that you should give alms or pray, but rather that you should give yourself entirely to your neighbor, as he needs and as you can, with alms, prayer, fasting, counsel, comfort, teaching, appeal, reproof, pardon, clothes, food, and also suffering and death on his behalf. But tell me, where in all Christendom are such works?

Would that I had a voice of thunder to resound throughout the world against that expression "good works," that it might be rooted out of heart, mind, ears, and books, or else correctly understood. A good work is called "good" because it is helpful and does good to him to whom it is done. What good is it to wear a costly robe or build a lordly mansion? What good is it to adorn churches with silver and gold and statues of stone or wood? What good if every hamlet had ten bells as big as those of Erfurt?

The Cleansing of the Temple (John 2:13–16)

In John's Gospel the cleansing of the Temple appears to come directly after the baptism of Christ, whereas in Matthew's Gospel it comes after the entry into Jerusalem on Palm Sunday. It is not important to settle this question. It may be that John has jumped over the entire interval from the beginning of Jesus' ministry to the last Passover because less interested in the deeds than in the words of Christ. Be that as it may. If you cannot contrive a reconciliation of John and Matthew, let it go. You won't be damned on that account.

The cleansing of the Temple presents a graver problem in that Christ, who was only a private person and not a civil ruler, behaved like a ruler. The prophet said that Messiah should smite the earth with a rod of his mouth. (Isa. 11:4.) This means that Christ should not have the sword in the hand because there it belongs to the magistrate. Rather, Christ's sword should be that which proceeds from the mouth, and the sword of the mouth is nothing other than the Word of God. But in that case, if the Kingdom of Christ is restricted to the sword of the mouth, why did Christ use the sword of the fist? I think it was a concession to the Old Testament just as when Christ allowed himself to be circumcised. Sometimes he followed Moses and sometimes rejected him. Sometimes he kept and sometimes broke the Sabbath. But in the New Testament the two jurisdictions are sharply distinguished. I, as a minister, have a spiritual rod in the mouth; you, as a magistrate, a physical rod in the fist. I am not to tell you how to punish and strike, nor are you to tell me how to preach. That would be overstepping your bounds.

"Let Not Your Heart Be Troubled" (John 14:1–14)

Here you see how warm, faithful, and friendly was the Lord Jesus to his disciples that he left them not without comfort on the very night on which he was to be taken from them through his bitter suffering and cross, and would leave them behind in danger, fear, and terror. While he had been with them, they were full of assurance. Now he let them know it would be different. Their hearts would be full of fright and dismay, as indeed it happened when he was so shamefully and cruelly done to death. This was not the Christ who had raised the dead and cleansed the Temple. Now he was weak and trampled under foot. Then the hearts of the disciples were congealed with fear and they dared nothing, but cried in anguish: "Oh, where shall we stay? He has been our comfort and defense, and now he is gone. There is no one now to protect us. Our enemies are strong and mighty, and we are abandoned by the world." That is why Christ spoke these words, to show them in advance the coming terror and to comfort them that they might remember and be upheld.

If then you would be a Christian like the apostles and the saints, arm yourselves, and be certain that someday an hour will come when your heart will be terrified and shaken. This is said to all Christians to make them realize that their present security will not last long. Today is tranquil; tomorrow will be different. The devil can strike a javelin into the heart, or some other distress will overtake you. See to it then that you are armed and take comfort from God's Word.

From this assurance we must learn and know what Christ is like. He is not one to strike terror and sorrow because he has come to take away terror and sorrow and to give instead a light heart and a free conscience. That is why he promised to send to his disciples the Holy Spirit, the Comforter. The Christian, then, may be subject outwardly to much suffering and distress, but at the same time can be comforted and joyful in heart and mind toward God. Let us learn that whatever misfortune may overtake us, be it pestilence, war, high prices, poverty, persecution, or dismal imaginations which smite the head and crush the heart, we may conclude that all of this is from Christ to guard us against the devil who can disguise himself with the very form and name of Christ.

"Ye Believe in God, Believe Also in Me" (John 14:1)

Up until now it has been said that the Holy Spirit rules the councils, determines the articles of faith, and confers papal decrees. This is the greatest dishonor that one can do to the Holy Spirit. This is to make the Holy Spirit into a dead law rather than a living principle written by the Spirit in the heart. The Holy Spirit comes down from heaven, fills men, and makes their tongues as flames of fire that they may fear nought.

Temples of God (John 14:23)

It is a great consolation that he will make his abode with us. Where God is, there is his temple. God's abode is where he speaks, works, and is found. This occurs in a true Christian man, and nothing is more precious. What is it to have temples of gold? We are enraged if the Turk destroys temples and altars, but in the meantime we destroy the true temples of God. We seek to defend with the sword temples of wood built by man and destroy man, the temple built by God.

"God So Loved the World" (John 3:16)

These are astounding words. God has every reason to be angry and to wipe out the world as a frightful enemy, and yet there is no greater lover than God and no more desperate scoundrel than the world. To love the world and wish it well is beyond me. If I were God, I would give it hell-fire. But instead of consuming the world in anger, God loves the world with such unspeakable and overflowing love that he gave his Son. My powers are not adequate to reach to the bottom of this tremendous affirmation. This love is greater than the fire seen by Moses [in the burning bush], greater even than the fire of hell. Who will despair if God so loves the world?

"That he gave his only-begotten son, that whosoever believeth in him should not perish, but have eternal life."

The words read so simply but are so mighty. They are greater than the heavens and the sun. God will give us eternal life. If he offered us a dukedom or a kingdom, we should dispute and say: "It cannot be. He would not give me a kingdom." We think we are not worth more than twenty gulden, for what is man compared with God? But see now what God has in mind, that he should not strangle, terrify, and harass mankind, but rather should give life, and even eternal life. Compare life with every other gift on earth. Would one give his life for the kingdom of France? Hardly, nor even for the whole world. But now God is going to give life which is better than all the treasures of the world, and not only life but eternal life. What is the reason? It is that God so loved the world. These are overwhelming words.

God's gifts are inexpressible. What does he give? His only begotten Son. This is not the gift of a groshen, an eye, a horse, a cow, or a kingdom. No, nor heaven with the sun and the stars, nor the whole creation, but his Son, who is as great as himself. This should kindle sheer light, yes, fire, in our hearts, that we should ever dance for joy. If God gives his Son, he withholds nothing, for he gives himself.

"All things are yours," as Paul says, "whether Paul or Apollos or Cephas, or the world, or life, or death, or things present, or things to come; all are yours; and ye are Christ's; and Christ is God's." (I Cor. 3:21–23.)

This treasure is not given as a reward. It is a gift. It is your own. You have only to accept it. It is not a castle, but God's Son who is given. Hold out your hand and take, but the world is so possessed of the devil as to be unwilling to be simply a receiver. God certainly has to be a great forgiver in order to forgive the world, which so reviles him. When, then, God gives so much to the world, gives indeed his very self, how can the world hate him? Think of what I have done myself! For fifteen years I said Mass, crucified Christ, and practiced idolatry in the cloister, and yet God sent his Son for me and forgave me everything. O Lord God, ought we not to rejoice and not only serve gladly but suffer and laugh at death *for* the sake of him who has given us such a treasure? If I believe this, should I not be willing to be burned at the stake?

"My Peace I Give unto You" (John 14:27)

When you are in the midst of suffering Christ says: "I will make you feel as if you were in paradise. In war I will give you peace; in death, life."

"When the Comforter Comes" (John 15:26)

That we fail not, Christ said, "I will send you a Comforter." When my sins and the fear of death affright me, then he comes and touches my heart and says: "For shame! Up again!" He breathes upon us a new spirit and speaks to us in a friendly and comforting way, that we should not quail before death even if we had ten necks but rather should say, "Even though I have sinned, I have come through and had I still enough sins to engulf me I would yet hope not to be hurt." This is not to say, of course, that we should not feel our sins, for the flesh must feel them, but the Spirit overcomes them and cows fear and despair. What then can the creature do against us if the Creator be for us?

All Shall Bear Witness (John 15:27)

It is not enough that we believe. We must also testify, and yet recognize that to do so lies beyond our power. The Lord gives the reason when he says, "They will put you under the ban" (John 16:2). If you wish to witness and say very much about Christ, you will have an adversary. Lucifer and his angels will swoop upon you like a thousand wolves about a sheep. When the devil sees you lighting a lamp to enlighten others he begins to rage. He can stand it better if you believe only for yourself. But if you want to kindle a light for others, you will be in danger of death, as we see by experience. This fulfills the word of Christ. "The time cometh, that whosoever killeth you will think he doeth God's service." (John 16:2.)

Asking the Father (John 16:23)

This is an exhortation to prayer in extreme anxiety. Certain it is that when there is no distress there is no prayer. Or if there is a prayer it is feeble and listless, without sap and drive. That is why troubles are so needful. It is better to suffer a trial than to own a house, for all the riches in the world are not to be compared with a severe trial. The reason is that when there is no trial we are complacent and do not ask nor seek after God, but when distress overtakes us we have two kinds of prayer. The first cannot be expressed, as when Paul spoke of "groanings unutterable" (Rom. 8:26). This prayer never ceases, and no one sees it save the one who makes it and even he does not know how deep it is. For example, when someone lies in prison for the gospel and is to be burned, he prays and prays so mightily that he himself has never known such powerful prayer. No one by tongue or pen can make a prayer as strong as this. Then comes the second kind of prayer, the outward, as when he who opens to a psalm derives comfort from it. What a relish he has for it! One sees in the heart of such a man pure humility and compassion for his enemies.

The Lord then will comfort those who make such prayers. No one can pray who has not known calamity. Prayers are unavailing which lack the great treasure, the holy cross.

"I Know My Sheep" (John 10:1–18)

We should be comforted that he calls us sheep. One person may lack gold, goods, health, another something else. It seems, then, as if we were in the jaws of the wolf and had no shepherd. By no means does it appear as if Christ so loved us. We see and feel quite

otherwise in life and death, but we must hear his whistle and learn to know him. "I am your shepherd; you are my sheep because you hear my voice. In this way you know me, and I know you." This knowledge is through faith.

6

The Lord's Supper

An Outward Sign

[1520]

Quite commonly God has given along with the word a sign as a further assurance and strengthening of faith. Noah was given the sign of the rainbow, Abraham of circumcision, Gideon of the dew upon the fleece. This happens when men make a will. There is not only a word but also a notary's seal to show that it is valid and

trustworthy, and so Christ in making his testament attached a seal and sign to the words, namely, his own true flesh and blood under the bread and wine.

Not an Untouchable Charm

[1522]

A Christian should know that there is on earth no greater holiness than God's Word. The Sacrament itself is made blessed and hallowed through God's Word by which we are all spiritually born and consecrated to Christ. If then a Christian with mouth, ears, heart, and the whole body may lay hold of the Word which hallows all things and is above the sacraments, why may he not touch that which is hallowed through the Word? Otherwise he should not so much as touch his own body, because he is himself as hallowed as the Sacrament. A Christian is holy in body and soul, whether layman or priest, man or woman. To say the contrary is to blaspheme holy Baptism, the blood of Christ, and the grace of the Holy Spirit. A Christian is great and rare, and God cares more about him than about the Sacrament, for the Christian is not made for the Sacrament, but the Sacrament for the Christian, and these blind heads want to dispute whether the Sacrament may be touched, and make a heresy out of so doing. Away with these hardened and infatuated heathen who do not know what a Christian is! God deliver us from them.

Inward and Unconstrained

[1522]

[Over against the position of the Roman Catholics, Luther constantly stressed the inwardness of the Sacrament.]

The outward and the inward partaking of the Sacrament are to be carefully distinguished. To take the elements is outward and that can be done without faith and love. If such reception made a Christian, then a mouse would be a Christian, for a mouse can nibble the bread and even sip the wine. The inner, spiritual, true reception is quite something else and consists in the use and the fruit, which take place in faith.

But not all people have this faith. For that reason no ordinance should be made out of this Sacrament like the silly requirement of the holy father, the pope, that everyone go to Mass at Easter on pain of being denied Christian burial. Is not that a foolish command? We are not all alike and do not have all the same faith. One has a stronger faith than another. For that reason there can be no general ordinance. It is because of this that at Easter the greatest sins are committed by unworthy participation, all on account of this unchristian command which seeks to drive and force people to the Sacrament. And why? Because the pope cannot see into the heart, whether faith be there or not. If you believe that God takes your part and gives his blood for you, if you believe that God says: "Follow me unaffrighted. Let us see what can harm you. Let the devil, death, sin, hell, and all creatures do their worst. If I am for you, if I am your guard and protector, trust me and follow boldly after me"-he who believes this belongs here and takes the Sacrament as an assurance, seal, or pardon, that he is certain of the divine assurance and promise. But such faith we do not all have. Would to God that one tenth of the people had it!

Everyone cannot have such a rich, overflowing treasure, with which out of grace we are showered by God. They alone possess it who have endured physical or spiritual torments in the body through persecution or in the spirit through a devastating conscience. When the devil outwardly or inwardly makes the heart weak, fearful, and crushed, so that it does not know how it stands with God, and sin looms before it, then in such a stricken heart God will dwell, for who needs a protector and guard if he has not gone through torment and his sins gnaw daily? In that case he does not belong at this table because this food calls for hungry and questing spirits. He who does not feel this should abstain for a time from the Sacrament because this food will not enter a satisfied and full heart, but if we sense qualms of conscience and the foreboding of a heart dismayed, then we shall come with all humility and reverence, not tripping and trotting. But we are not always in the mood. Today I have grace and I am ready, but tomorrow, no. Perhaps six months from now I shall have no desire or readiness. They are best prepared who are always beset by death and the devil. They are the very ones who are most likely to have the faith that nothing can harm them, because they have in themselves that which no one can take away. That is why, when Christ instituted the Sacrament, he first dismayed his disciples when he told them that he would go away from them, and he cut them deeply when he said that one of them would betray him. Do you not think that these words went to their very hearts? They must have been appalled and sat there as if every one of them had betrayed God, and only when Christ saw them tremble, quake, and quail did he institute the Holy Sacrament to their comfort. Wherefore, the bread is a consolation to the troubled and medicine for the sick, life for the dying, food for the hungry, and a rich treasure for the poor and needy.

Sufficient for today on the use of the Sacrament, I commend you to God.

Also Outward

[1525]

No one can deny that the three Evangelists, Matthew, Mark, and Luke, and also Paul, say that Christ took the bread and blessed it and broke it and gave it to his disciples saying, "Take eat, this is my body which is broken for you." And again the cup, saying, "This is my blood of the new covenant." Then in addition to these four powerful passages there is another in I Cor. 10:16: "The cup of blessing, which we bless, is it not a communion of the blood of Christ? The bread which we break, is it not a communion of the body of Christ?" There's a thunderclap for Dr. Carlstadt. Do you hear this, my dear brother? The bread broken and distributed in pieces is a communion of the body of Christ. It is, it is, it is, says Paul, a communion of the body of Christ. But what is the communion of the body of Christ? It could not be anything other than that those who take the broken bread, each one a piece, receive in it the body of Christ. This communion means to participate in the body of Christ, so that each one with the other receives the common body of Christ. Paul says that we are all one body, and we all partake of one bread. That is why it has long been called the Communion, that is, a fellowship.

Here Dr. Carlstadt performs gymnastics to get away from the sense of this text. He employs his perverted trick of interpreting only in a spiritual and inward sense that which God has instituted physically and outwardly, and, on the other hand, of making outward and physical that which God has made inward and spiritual. He takes the word "communion" and says this means only spiritual communion, so that the communion of the body of Christ means that we reflect upon and share his suffering.

But communion with the suffering of Christ cannot be a communion with the flesh and blood of Christ because anyone who would suffer with Christ or participate in his sufferings must be godly, spiritual, and believing. A sinful, fleshly man could not do that, but even the unworthy can partake in the body of Christ, as Paul says (I Cor. 11:29), "He that eateth and drinketh unworthily, eateth and drinketh damnation to himself." That is what happened to Judas. With all the other disciples at the Last Supper, he partook of the body and the blood of Christ. He received it and ate and drank just as much as the others.

My dear friend, the natural meaning of language is an empress, and goes far beyond any subtle, hair-splitting, sophisticated interpretation. One must not depart from the natural sense unless an obvious article of faith compel it, otherwise no letter of the Scripture will be safe from these crystal-gazers.

Christ's Body Not in Heaven

[1527]

But we are told that Christ is not bodily in the Sacrament because he ascended into heaven and sits at the right hand of God. When we read this we are not to think of a cardboard heaven such as children like to color and put in it a golden chair with Christ sitting beside the Father wearing a chorister's cape or a golden crown. If it were not for such pictures, there would not be so much dispute nor such insistence that Christ must be in a particular locality.

The right hand of God is not a place, because God is essentially present in all the ends of the earth, in and through all creatures. We know that God's arm, hand, face, spirit, and wisdom are all the same thing. We know that the whole Godhead dwells bodily in Christ (Col. 2:9). How, then, can it also be true that God was in Christ essentially and personally on earth in the womb, in the cradle, in the Temple, in the wilderness, in the town and villages and gardens and fields, on the cross, in the grave—and at the same time in heaven in the bosom of the Father? If, now, according to our faith, it is true that the Godhead was essentially and personally present in Christ on earth in so many places, and at the same time in heaven and with the Father, then we must conclude that the Godhead is everywhere present and essentially and personally fills heaven and earth and everything with his nature and majesty, as Jeremiah says (Jer. 23:23–24), "I fill heaven and earth and am a God who is near," and the Psalmist says (Ps. 139:7), "Who can flee from his presence?"

For this reason, if Christ had never spoken the words at the Lord's Supper, "This is my body," nevertheless the saying that Christ sits at the right hand of God shows that his body and blood can be there and also in all other places at the same time. There is no need here for any transubstantiation or any transformation of the bread into his body. He can be there without all this because the right hand of God does not have to be first changed into all things in which it is present. We are not so crude as to suppose that Christ's body is in the bread in so crass and visible a manner as bread is in a basket or wine is in a jar, as the Radicals claim we do. We believe that his body is there, as the words say: "This is my body." We do not care about the expression. We are ready to say he is in the bread, he is where the bread is, or as you will. We will not quarrel about words so long as this remains—that this is not ordinary bread which we eat in the Lord's Supper, but it is the body of Christ.

Why not, then, eat the body of Christ anywhere because he is everywhere present? Because you are not to try to eat him as you would eat sauerkraut and soup on your table, but only where he wishes. He is not to be seized, and you will not lay hold of him, even if he is in your bread, unless he binds himself to you and brings himself through his word to the particular table, that you partake of him there.

Do Not Worry Or Pry Into the Inscrutable
[1534]

Christians should do God honor and believe that he can do what he says. They should not be like the Radicals who trouble themselves to know how bread can be body and wine can be blood. They want to comprehend God, and because this does not agree with reason, they assume that God cannot do it; but why should man torment himself to death to make everything agree with reason? If it is God's word, he is almighty and true. Then, we should accept in faith, simply, like children. We should be thankful and joyous and ask for what purpose he has done it—not whether he can. There is no man among us who knows how the eye sees, how we go to sleep, and how we wake up. The voice of the preacher fills several thousand ears and hearts. I see it and hear it but do not understand it. We want to be masters and judges in matters which are hidden from us, and we do not understand our daily life. What happens that the tongue moves in the mouth to make speech? No man can tell you how a hair grows. If then, we cannot grasp that in which we live and move, how shall we comprehend that which God alone discloses and in which we do not live? You can judge that your cow eats hay and grass. Gold, silver, stone, and corn—all this reason can handle—but what God does with the tongue, the eyes, and the ears, you will have to leave undisputed. The thing for you to ask is whether God or man has spoken and whether it is a work of God or of man. If it is God's word and work, then shut your eyes and do not ask how it happens. I should be baptized and become pure from all my sins. That is his word. So also here: come, eat, "do this in remembrance of me." This is his true flesh and blood because his Word says so, and not that of a man. He has instituted it and commanded it. Baptism in his sacrament and work. I feel and hear well enough what he says, but what takes place I do not know. Do not give yourself over, then, to questions and disputes, but consider the use and the joy of the Sacrament.

He has made it as easy and as lovable as possible. Whether you stand or sit does not matter. He has laid no hard work upon us. Eating and drinking is the easiest thing. There is nothing men would rather do. It is the most joyous exercise on earth. As the proverb says, "No dancing before eating," or again, "A happy head crowns a full stomach." He invites you to a sweet and friendly meal and will lay no heavy burden upon you. There is nothing about cowls, nothing about pilgrimages in armor to Jerusalem, circumcision, sacrifices of animals, and ablutions as in the law, but he says: "You have the Lord's Supper. When you come together and would learn of me, take bread and wine and repeat the words, 'This is my body and blood.'"

[1519]

From all this it is clear that the Sacrament is nothing other than a divine sign whereby Christ and all saints with all their works, sufferings, merits, graces, and goods are given as consolation and strength to all who are sore beset by the devil, sin, the world, the flesh, and all evil. To receive the Sacrament is to believe this, for everything depends on faith. It is not enough to know what the Sacrament is and means. You must believe that you have received it. There are those who puzzle themselves as to how the whole of Christ's body and blood can be present in such a tiny piece of bread and sip of wine. You do not need to be concerned about that. It is enough if you know that this is a divine sign and that Christ's flesh and blood are truly here. How and where they are present you may leave to him. When you are downcast be assured that in this Sacrament, Christ and all saints come to you with all their virtues, suffering, and grace. They live, suffer, and die with you and seek to be wholly yours and to share in all things with you. If you will exercise and increase this faith, you will experience what a joyous marriage feast your God has prepared for you upon the altar.

Let the Unexamined Abstain

[1523]

This year, once more, we shall allow each to come to the Sacrament according to his own judgment, but in the future no one will be admitted who has not first been examined and declared how his heart stands, whether he knows what the Sacrament is, and why he comes.

But the Timorous Are Invited

[1528]

Now that we have a proper understanding and doctrine of the Sacrament, a word of exhortation is in order that this great treasure, which is daily dispensed among Christians, should not be neglected. Those who are Christians should dispose themselves to partake often. There are a great many who, now that we are freed from the pope, will go for one, two, or three years and even longer without the Sacrament, as if they were such strong Christians that they did not need it. Some, again, are deterred because we have taught that they only should come who are driven by hunger and thirst. Some even say that it is free and not necessary and it is enough if one believes. The greater part are callous and despise alike God's Word and the Sacrament. Now it is true that we said none should be compelled and the Sacrament should not be made into soul torture. At the same time these folk should recognize that those who for so long a time abstain are not to be regarded as Christians, for Christ did not institute the Lord's Supper as a spectacle to be gazed upon, but as a supper to eat, drink, and remember.

I know from experience, and anyone can find it out for himself, that if one does stay away from day to day, one will grow more callous and cold and in the end will be carried away by the wind. One should examine the heart and conscience and see whether one is of those who desire to be right with God. The more that happens, the more will the heart be warm and kindled.

[1529]

But you say, "I am not worthy." Well, that is my temptation too. You heard in the papists' sermons that we should be entirely pure, without a blemish. That is why we are so timorous, and the heart at once says, "I am not worthy"; so I decide to wait until the next Sunday, until I am better; and the next Sunday goes over to the next, and so on till the quarter of the year, and the half, and the whole. But if I waited until I were entirely pure and had no more reproaches of conscience, I should in that case never come, or not for a very long time.

A distinction is to be made, however, in the case of brazen sinners guilty of adultery, usury, extortion, theft, public hate, or envy. To such rough, wild persons one should say, "Stay away." They are not ready for the forgiveness of sins. They wish to remain evil.

But if your sins are not such that they should be publicly reproved by the congregation, you should not abstain, but should say to yourself: "I do not come in my own righteousness. In that case I would never come. A child is not baptized because it is godly, and I do not go to confession because I am pure. I go as one who is unworthy, who cannot be worthy. God preserve me from being worthy." We are always looking at our hands rather than at Christ's mouth. We ought to say, "I see what thou sayest, not what I do."

[1534]

Strange that some are afraid of the Sacrament! The peasants are troubled because they think they must have left all their sins. No wonder that under the papacy the people took it so hard! The papists have corrupted the Sacrament with gall, vinegar, and wormwood, and taken all the joy out of it, for we were taught that we must be so pure that not one fleck of the least sin should remain upon us, and so holy that for sheer holiness our Lord God could not look upon us. I was not able to find that in myself, and on that account I was terrified and I am still plagued by this residue from the papacy, but now joy is coming back. Of course, it is true that we should be godly, and if you love your sins more than God's grace, stay way. But the Lord's Supper is a sweet, savory food, from which you are not to derive poison and death. Listen, it is given for you, not against you. For your soul's comfort, strength, and redemption was it given. Christ does not put you under the water of baptism in order to drown you, but that you may be saved from your sins and likewise in the Lord's Supper. That is why you should learn the use and the purpose. Here Christ has established the Sacrament for you and for me. I feel that I am a scoundrel, that the devil has taken hold of me, that I do not do what I should. People in this case ought to be invited to take the Sacrament. They should not dread it as a frightful judgment. That feeling arises from the old custom or from the devil, but Christians should come with joy and confidence and think: "I will eat his flesh and blood. Why has he given them to me? Surely he will not cast me off if I seek only in his name to be blessed and look for help and comfort."

The Sacrament of Love

[1522]

Yesterday we heard about the true use of the Holy Sacrament. Now we come to the fruit of this Sacrament, namely, love, that we may behave toward our neighbor as God toward us. From God we have received nothing but love and kindness, for Christ has given his all for us, which no angel can comprehend, for God is a glowing bake oven full of love that reaches from earth to heaven. Love, I say, is the fruit of this Sacrament, but as yet I see little of it here at Wittenberg, though there has been much preaching about it. Love is the greatest, but nobody attends to it above all else, but rather to that which does not matter. Paul says, "If I speak with the tongues of men and of angels, and have not love, I am become a sounding brass and a tinkling cymbal." Those are terrifying words of Paul's. "And if I have all wisdom and all knowledge to understand God's secrets, if I have faith so as to move mountains and have not love, it is nothing. And if I give my goods to feed the poor and my body to be burned, and have not love, it profiteth nothing." There is nobody here who has given all his goods to feed the poor nor his body to be burned, and yet even these, without love, are nothing. But you want to receive everything from God in the Sacrament, and you do not wish to pour out again in love. No one will give a hand to another and everyone is thinking about himself. Nobody bothers about the poor.

You have heard enough on this for a long time back. All my books are full of urging faith and love. If you do not love one another, God will let loose a great plague upon you. He will not have his word preached in vain. You tempt God too much, my friends. If these words had been preached to our fathers, they might have responded differently, and if now one went to preach in this fashion to many in the cloisters, they would accept it more joyously, but you do not take this to heart. Instead, you go gawking after some trumpery. I commend you to God.

Fellowship

[1519]

The meaning of this Sacrament is the communion of all saints. The participation in bread and wine is the sign of fellowship with Christ and all the saints just as a man on becoming a citizen is given a certificate testifying that he belongs to a town and a community. When you share in this Sacrament you must take to yourself all that may befall the community. Give your heart over to love and learn that this is a sacrament of love. In all its forms it suggests and kindles fellowship. Just as grains of wheat are kneaded together and assume one form in the bread, just as grapes and berries when pressed give up their individual shapes and become a common body, so should Christians be a single spiritual body.

[1528]

I have the same faith, teaching, and Sacrament with you. Likewise I have the same weakness, ignorance, transgressions, and poverty with you. Are you naked? Then am I also, and I can have no peace until I have clothed you. Are you hungry and thirsty? Thus we come into one kitchen and my food is yours and your hunger and thirst are mine. Again, are you a sinner? Then so am I. Or am I joyous and strong? Then I take on your sadness and weakness and rest not until you are like me. Thus, your joy is my joy and likewise, your sadness is mine.

[1519]

Christ with all his saints assumes in love our form and fights with us against sin, death, and all evil. Thereby, we are kindled and assume his form, abandoning ourselves to his righteousness, being kneaded into the fellowship of his benefits and of our miseries as one loaf, one body, and one drink. How great a Sacrament this is, as Paul says, that Christ should be one flesh and one bone with his church. (Eph. 5:32.) So ought we also in the same love to transform ourselves and take to ourselves the needs and the transgressions of other Christians, and whatever we have of good, we should leave to them that they may also enjoy it. Then we shall be made over into each other and fashioned into a fellowship of love without which this change cannot take place.

7

Arrest and Trial

On What to Meditate

Today is Passion Sunday. It is good once a year to read through the whole story of the Passion. If I go for two days without thinking of Christ, I become faint and sluggish. What, then, would become of those who for a year at a time do not hear of him?

Yet, even those who hear the Word are not awakened. The Passion of Christ has been read, sung, and preached, but to what end? One may say that it is both proclaimed and hidden. Few of those who gladly hear reflect upon the meaning. They go to church, listen to the recital of the Passion, and as they came in, so they go out. They are delighted to hear that Christ our Lord shed his blood for us, but should we tell them not to covet, to grasp, to fornicate—then the whole Rhine would be ablaze. They retort: "You should not scold us. We are all Christians. God has saved us from our sins." Thus, a particle of candid truth stirs up resentment. Such is the nature of this preaching—that though it is publicly proclaimed, scarcely does it ever lodge in the heart.

The Gospels are discrepant with regard to the external events in the garden of Gethsemane. The frivolous fasten on details of this sort and lose the essentials. If, for example, we concentrate on the crown of thorns, the nails, and the pieces of the cross, we miss the true use of the Passion. I wish the cross had never been discovered, and perhaps it is not genuine, for the devil is fond of drawing us from Christ to a piece of wood. I really believe that the story of the finding of the true cross is all made up. I wish, also, that the bones of Christ and of all saints were under the earth in some unknown place like those of Moses. Let us then center on Christ and not bother about the Jews, the house, the supper, Judas, and the arrest. You do not need to go to Jerusalem and look at the footprints of Jesus. What good is it to have seen the house of Pilate or the steps on which Christ fainted? The question is how Christ looks upon you.

"The chief priests and the scribes sought how they might take him by craft, and put him to death. But they said, Not on the feast day, lest there be an uproar of the people." (Mark 14:1-2.)

They were afraid to do it at the time of the feast when so many Jews came up to Jerusalem. They would make thirty times one hundred thousand, without women and children. I doubt whether there are so many people in all Germany. So, the chief priests said: "See how the people hang upon him. We shall have to be crafty and strike at the right time if the plot is to succeed."

Anointing in Bethany (Mark 14:3-9)

On the eve prior to Passion Week, Jesus was in Bethany. We read that Mary took ointment. It was an old custom to wash with perfumed water not only the face but also the hands and the feet. Mary had purchased a very costly vessel. In our day we have wild nard, but not the kind mixed with balsam of that time, which was very precious. It was not an ointment but a sweet, smelling perfume with herbs. She poured it over his head and raiment. It spoiled nothing but made everything pure and of a sweet smell. The Lord suffered it. He took no pleasure in the perfume, for his heart was full of heaviness and thoughts of death. In six days, he would die. He who knows certainly that he will die a shameful death on a particular day will take no delight in gold, pearl necklaces, and clothes, for his spirit is in deep anguish because he must shed his blood. Piping, singing, and dancing do not help here. But Christ permitted what she did. Mary believed him to be a prophet and meant it well. He was wrestling with death and took no delight in this of itself.

Then Judas Iscariot, the son of Simon, thought to himself: "Mary wastes money. She pours out the perfume even on his feet and this rose water costs so much. Why did she not use lye or soap?

This perfume might have been sold for three hundred groschen and given to the poor." A groschen, by the way, corresponded to a Nuremberg pound and came to about thirty-five gulden. Judas probably said to himself: "That is too much. With this amount of money I could have fed twenty-four people and could indeed have cared for sixty persons for a month, and now it is all gone in one hour." This all sounds very plausible, and it is just the way the pope raises money to go against the Turks. Now, of course, fighting the Turks and giving alms to the poor are good, but the pope means it like Judas.

Christ said: "Let her alone. . . . She is come aforehand to anoint my body to the burying." He pointed to his death, though she did not understand it. These thirty-five gulden, he would say, are a farewell. If it were for the last time, I would give all at once every thing that I might have given in thirty years as a token of love to Christ's Word.

Washing of the Disciples' Feet (John 13:1–20)

Christ sent the disciples into the city to prepare the Passover supper for him. And when they were gathered, he took "a basin, and began to wash the disciples' feet." In this, one sees what a person he was; how inconceivably friendly. "Ye call me Master and Lord," he said, "and ye say well; for so I am. If I then, your Lord and Master, have washed your feet; ye also ought to wash one another's feet."

There was no need that Christ should have done this. He could have said to Peter, "You go and wash Judas' feet; I am the Master." But instead he subjected himself and emptied himself of his majesty and behaved as a servant. Then Peter undertook to instruct him and said, "You are the Master, and I am the servant," but Christ rebuffed him and went on to explain the meaning of the foot washing.

What a contrast between Christ washing the disciples' feet and the pope having his toe kissed! Christ well foresaw that the successors of the apostles would wish to receive service, but he intended that all Christians and, especially the successors of the apostles, should render service. This does not refer specifically to foot washing, though I like it and would gladly have it continued, but when it comes to theatrical foot washing, that is sheer ostentation.

The pope, the Cardinal of Mainz, and King Ferdinand make a ceremony of washing a beggar's feet. (I wish them all to the devil!) They will hang a man and on the same day wash feet in imitation of Christ. If I were God, I would smite them with thunder and lightning. Still, I was proud enough myself when I was a monk. If, then, you really want to wash the feet of the poor, take them into your house, feed them, and clothe them, and do it the whole year through.

In washing the feet of the disciples, Christ gave an example of love, for this is the nature of love—to serve and to be subject to another. If one esteems another more highly than himself, then love and all good works are there. Jesus said, "Ye also ought to wash one another's feet." Thus Christ made himself the lowliest. One sees here genuine love, for the heart is with the loved one and desires to do his pleasure. In this, one finds sympathy, mercy, brotherliness, and a helping hand, but then the devil breaks in and says through the pope that these are not enough; that they are just ordinary commands; that one should go farther, become a monk, put on a cowl, and fast for six days. Even faith is called an ordinary thing, and we are told to do something extraordinary. Faith is merely for the heathen, but Christians must be urged to do something more, to take a cowl and the like. As for myself, I have scarcely made a beginning in faith. To the very grave, I

shall have to go on learning. I am not concerned about works. I pray simply, "Help me that I may firmly believe." If that happens, then bring on all the cowls and everything else the pope has commanded. So, then, love your neighbor and esteem him higher than yourself. But then again they come and say that this is only an ordinary command. I reply: "Where are those who have kept it? Have you? You have not."

It is a mighty love that puts us all to confusion that the divine majesty should so humble himself. Fie, how shameful if we do not take it to heart! But who knows whether his heart is pure. Look at Judas. There he sits like a lord full of the devil. And the Lord God goes down on his knees as a servant in front of him. If the kaiser should kiss a beggar's feet, that would be a stinking humility and not worthy to be named in comparison with what was done by the divine majesty. These examples are too deep for us to think of imitating.

Gethsemane

After the supper, we read in John's Gospel (John 18:1) that "he went forth with his disciples over the brook Cedron, where was a garden." This was the Garden of Gethsemane. Why did Jesus not flee? He did not evade the cross. He could have done so sevenfold, but he continued his way according to his custom. From this we see that one should neither seek nor shun the cross. No one has been given his body in order to crucify it. In that case, God would not have made the body healthy. The purpose of the body is to labor as a servant in order to provide food, clothes, work, and rest. The body is to be kept in subjection, but we are not to court affliction.

"And Judas also, who betrayed him, knew the place." Judas, then, having received a band of men and officers from the chief priests, came thither. Judas had two bands, one from the priests, the other from the Romans, that none might call him a rebel. Christ was then abandoned by the angels and by the authorities, and even his disciples fled. How was everything reversed! When he preached in Jerusalem, no one dared to touch him. Now the people and the magistrates forsook him. That is the way it is bound to be. If our Saxon princes were overcome and Wittenberg were besieged, we should then find out who were good Christians. Those who now are Evangelical would certainly desert and go over to the enemy, as the people then did to the Pharisees. He who would be a Christian must seek help that he may be strong in himself.

"Then Simon Peter having a sword drew it." (John 18:10–11.)

All too readily men grasp a sword. They forget how great a difference there is between the one to whom a thing is commanded and him to whom it is not. God does not slumber. He knows how government is to be conducted. When injustice occurs the mob is disposed to step in because the old Adam is a great fool. That is what Müntzer did. Peter had the best intentions. He was moved by love and loyalty to his Master. He said, "My Lord is in danger; I am his sworn disciple." The world could not blame him for that, but Christ did, as if to say: "There is a government in Jerusalem. They will deal with this fellow. The sword has not been given to you."

Now as a matter of fact, the government did wrong, and Peter did right. Whom should I then commend, the one who had the authority and did wrong? Obviously not, but also not the one who having no authority did right. Even if you could raise the dead, the sword would not on that account be committed to you. Here is the word, "Put up thy sword into the sheath." Of course, it is true that Peter was defending an innocent man and that he had the best of intentions, but you must leave questions of right to the jurists and inquire what has been committed to you. Christ would rather suffer wrong than overturn God's order, and God would rather have an

Arrest and Trial

unjust magistracy than an unjust people. The reason is that the mob gets out of hand and heads fly in all directions. That is why Peter, despite his good intentions, was wrong, and Pilate, the Pharisees,

and the godless were right. The peasants had the very best case when they said, "Who can stand for this?" But they ought also to have said, "We have not received the command." You have no business to say: "My heart is right. My intentions are good; the case is just." But rather you should say, "Have I been commissioned?" Unfortunately in the world everything is upside down. Those who have the good intentions have not the authority, and those who have the authority have not the good intentions.

Trial Before Annas and Peter's Denial

Jesus was taken first to the house of Annas. Now Annas had a daughter given to Caiaphas to wife. She was the first woman in Jerusalem, and Caiaphas was a bigwig and, at that time, the high priest. As for rank, I would rather have been Caiaphas than the pope at Rome. But now let us come to theology. If Caiaphas could not be believed, then let the devil believe the papists, the councils, and the bishops. The moral is that you cannot believe anyone because of his high station. The jurists have boasted of their pope, that such loftiness cannot err, but take Caiaphas. He had a higher place than the pope and the emperor, but not only was he wrong and Annas with him, but they were the worst idiots on earth, for they crucified the Son of God.

"And Simon Peter followed Jesus." (John 18:15.)

I believe that in the whole story of the Passion no part is so carefully portrayed as Peter's denial, and there is a good reason, for no article is so hard to believe as the forgiveness of sins. That is because the other articles do not affect us, as for example, "I believe in God the Father Almighty" and so on, but the forgiveness of sins touches me and touches you. There are other articles that are hard to understand, as that the bread is his body or that the Holy Spirit appeared at the baptism, but this one is the hardest. Because it is so hard and a man is so terrified by hell and judgment, therefore the forgiveness of sins had to be drastically portrayed in Peter, that every man might take comfort.

"One of the officers struck Jesus with the palm of his hand . . . and Jesus answered, Why smitest thou me?" (John 18:22-23.)

This text has been utilized to turn God's command into a counsel of perfection. In the Sermon on the Mount, Jesus said, "If anyone strike thee on the one cheek, turn to him the other also, etc." This is the command of the gospel, that one should not resist evil nor avenge oneself. But now the cloisters and the universities have interpreted this as if it were not a command but only good advice. He who is so inclined, say they, may keep it, for it is merely counsel and not a binding word. By way of corroboration they adduce this text and say: "Did Christ turn the other cheek? Did he not rather reprove the servant? Therefore, the injunction to turn the other cheek is no command, for in that case, Jesus would have done it."

The apparent discrepancy is to be understood in terms of the two kingdoms, the civil and the spiritual. In the one the emperor rules over rascals. In the other the Son of God over Christians. Christ will accept only those whose hearts are right, for he has only the word and no rod or sword, but the civil government has to do with rascals. When they do wrong, they have to be constrained by blows. Otherwise no one could be safe in his own house. When one commits a crime the executioner must take off his head. Christ, then, means to say, "My teaching does not apply to the emperor, but only to the children of God." It was to these that he gave his teaching about turning the other cheek, giving away the cloak, and going the second mile, that is to say, overcoming evil with good. The word of Christ is advice when addressed to the world and the emperor, but when spoken to the Christian in the realm of the spirit, it is a command.

You reply, "But Christ did not follow this command; instead he said, 'Why do you strike me?'" But examine now this text more carefully and observe that Christ offered not merely the other cheek but his whole body to be scourged and crucified. Turning the other cheek and reproving in words are quite distinct. A Christian must suffer, but the word is placed in his mouth that he should declare what is unjust. If a robber assailed me in the woods and said, "Your cloak is mine," I should not agree with him, for in that case I should share his crime. The hand and the mouth need to be distinguished. The hand may give, but the mouth cannot approve.

Similarly when the world condemns our teaching and would take our lives, what, then, are we to do? Like Christ we should suffer not merely a blow on the cheek but burning itself, but if we say to the judge, "You are right in burning us," that would be to betray Christ and deny everything for which he died. As for my person, I will suffer, but as for my teaching I am unafraid. This Scripture is an example that we should be bold. The hang man may be my master, but my teaching is right. That is what Jesus said to the servant, and that is what we should say to the tyrants. This gripes the devil and wrings him as if he had been robbed of the half of hell.

Trial Before Pilate (John 18:28 to 19:16)

And Pilate said, "What accusation bring ye against this man?"

The accusers were convicted not only by their own consciences but by this very heathen. I would not exchange this comfort for ten Turkish empires. When Pilate asked, "What accusation bring ye against this man?" their consciences writhed. That is what happens in our case. Our opponents resist the truth and cry out against us, but if there were a proper hearing, our innocence would come to light. The Jews did present an accusation, namely, that Jesus claimed to be their king. That was the only charge which Pilate took seriously. The worst scoundrels could not have devised a more damaging accusation, just as today the gospel is said to be insurrectionary. The rascals knew the charge was not true that Christ desired to be a king. This is our comfort, that our Lord had to endure the charge of insurrection because of his word.

Pilate called Jesus and said, "Art thou the King of the Jews?" Jesus answered him, "Sayest thou this of thyself, or did others tell thee of me?" This sounds proud, but it was not. Jesus was denying the accusation. It was as if he said: "You know yourself, Pilate, whether I am a king, that is, whether I am a rebel. I call your conscience to witness. You did not say this of yourself, for your own eyes give the answer. You see that I am bound. I have no crowd about me ready to unsheath weapons. I have the air of a prisoner." Pilate was somewhat irritated at this answer though it was necessary and not proud, and this is the way in which I must talk to the emperor, "Does your Majesty say this of yourself or did someone else tell it to you?"

Pilate answered: "Am I a Jew? Thine own nation and the chief priests have delivered thee unto me: what hast thou done?" Then the Lord gave the finest and the clearest answer: "My Kingdom does no harm to you nor to the emperor. I am no rebel. That you can see with your own eyes and no one can say anything to the contrary."

Then Jesus made his confession, "My Kingdom is not of this world." That was a very dangerous confession, for at the very same time he both denied and confessed that he was a king. He admitted that he came to make a revolution and yet was not a revolutionary,

for the gospel does not come without revolution. "Think you that I am come to bring peace on earth?" He said, "I say, no, but division."

In just the same fashion we are revolutionists now. We preach that everyone should obey his lord and in this we are peaceful and peaceable. We teach and pray for peace. We help the emperor in his kingdom and then we upset his kingdom when we say that the Kingdom of Christ is higher than the kingdom of the Emperor Charles. Life and goods we submit in obedience, but we preach the gospel and this divides hearts from hearts. In this comes the revolution, that the father has a different faith from the son, not that they live in different houses, for Christ did not say, "I will send a fire and burn their houses down," but rather that in the same house there should be division. The point is not that children should not obey their parents but that they will believe differently. The gospel is a kingdom, and it effects a revolution, only it is a spiritual revolution.

Pilate said: "Ye have a custom, that I should release unto you one at the passover: will ye therefore that I release unto you the King of the Jews? Then cried they all again, saying, Not this man, but Barabbas." So is it today. Barabbas is made a town counselor, a bishop, a dean, and a provost. You cannot expect the world to be any different from what it was in Christ's day. We are serving in an inn where the devil is the keeper, the world is his wife, the lusts of the world are the household, and all of them put together are against the gospel. It is a shame that the world prefers murder, adultery, faithlessness, trickery, guile, lying, and deception to the truth. They would rather bathe the world in blood than have the truth.

"Then Pilate therefore took Jesus, and scourged him. And the soldiers platted a crown of thorns, and put it on his head, and they put on him a purple robe."

These soldiers did more than was commanded them. Scourging was the practice, but in addition, to please the priests, they gave him a crown of thorns, dressed him in a purple robe, and hailed him as King of the Jews because of his confession that he was a king. So they had a vaudeville giving him a crown and the imperial purple. What more cruel, biting, venomous, devilish mockery could they have devised! And that is what happens to the gospel now and ever will. Scourging hurts, but taunts cut deeper.

"Pilate therefore went forth again, and saith unto them, Behold, I bring him forth to you, that ye may know that I find no fault in him."

This is an invincible witness of the truth for Jesus, that Pilate confessed once, twice, thrice, yes, even six times that he found no fault in him. Likewise, we today should have such a teaching that our opponents will have to say, "It is indeed right, though we will have none of it."

"The Jews answered him, We have a law, and by our law he ought to die, because he made himself the Son of God."

Then Pilate trembled the more. It was not that he believed him to be the Son of God, but he thought: "The Romans do have many gods. Who knows?" We find that the heathen often claimed gods to have appeared in human form. So now Pilate thought, "Suppose he is a

Arrest and Trial

god?" He said then to Jesus: "Who art thou? Whence art thou?" But Jesus gave him no answer.

"Then saith Pilate unto him, Speakest thou not unto me? knowest thou not that I have power?"

Pilate trusted to and boasted in his might like a heathen. Similarly today there are those who want power to make and to break in the church according to their will. Christ now could no longer be silent. Where speech seemed timely, he spoke not, but where silence appeared seemly, he spoke. When Pilate claimed power, then Jesus told him he had no power. "Thou couldst have no power at all against me, were it not given thee from above." By this, Christ showed that one should not be silent in declaring the truth before the big lords. Christ did not, however, say, "Pilate, you have no power over me." Rather he said: "You have power, as you yourself say, but there is another point. You do not have it from yourself but it is given to you." In this, Christ reproved Pilate because he was so overweening and this we, too, must do to our Pilates. We are accused of despising the majesty of the emperor and the princes, but when they tell us we ought to say, "Gracious lord, what you do is right," that we will not do. There is a great difference between suffering injustice and in keeping still. Suffer, yes—be silent, no—for I must witness to the truth, and if we must die for the truth, still we must confess and reprove the lie with the mouth. If we say, "Dear lords, you are not behaving like Christian princes and spiritual fathers but rather like murderous apostates from Christ and enemies of the gospel"-if we say this, we are accused of treason, but I must speak. This is the truth. He who speaks against it is against God. He who goes against it is an enemy of the gospel.

Now if Pilate had had a grain of courage, he would have freed Jesus. Nature and reason teach that one should not do wrong for someone else. It will not do to say: "I stole your cow but not for myself. I did it for your enemy." So here Pilate manifestly did wrong for the sake of the Jews. Yet, he did try to set Jesus free, but the Jews said, "Let this man go, and thou art not Caesar's friend." The Jews had first claimed that Jesus was disloyal because he wanted to be a king. Pilate saw through this. Then they charged that Christ made himself out to be the Son of God. That, too, was unimpressive. Now they reverted to the first charge and heightened it by saying that if he wants to be a king, he is against the emperor, and if you set him free, we will write to Rome and accuse you of favoring a rebel.

Then Pilate wilted. "Thou art not Caesar's friend." That is the word that causes men to fall away like autumn leaves. Flesh and blood cannot bear to be the emperor's enemy. This made Pilate blind. So today there are many good Evangelicals, but they do not care enough for the gospel to risk limb and life. They follow Pilate. He has many children. Pilate then asked no more questions but passed judgment, saying to the Jews, "Behold your king!" He was saying as it were: "Fie, shame on you all! If you were the right sort, you would come armed to drive me and all my men out of your city because I crucified your king. You ought to defend him against me, but you drag him in, that I may execute him when I would rather set him free." Matthew records that Pilate washed his hands and said, "I am innocent of his blood." Yet, he turned him over to their will. He shared their guilt, even though he confessed Christ's innocence. The justice of the world can do no better.

Christ then was condemned not on account of his teaching but as a rebel against the imperial majesty, and he who would follow the gospel must endure the charge of revolution.

8

The Crucifixion

Then, "bearing his cross, he went forth." (John 19:17.)

So John records. The other Gospels say the Master could go no farther, and Simon of Cyrene was compelled to carry the cross for him. The painters who show Simon helping him are mistaken. Christ carried the cross himself to the gate, and from then on Simon took over. We are not so cruel as were the Orientals, for we do not make criminals carry their wheels, but this is written to show the great cost of the

redemption of our sins. Christ was not simply condemned but had even to carry the very cross on which he should die.

He went forth to a spot called Golgotha, the place of the skull—in Latin, *Calvary*. At Wittenberg, we call it the gallows. It was the common place of execution. Not only had he to carry his cross but also to be executed with two criminals—highway bandits, murderers who today are executed with the sword and wheel as breakers of the peace. Christ must be crucified not only with them but between them. Pilate did not command this, but the soldiers did it to please the high priest. There hung the Lord, a robber, a thief, a rebel, a murderer. All this the unspotted Lamb must bear, and all this was for us. Our sins lay upon his head and through him many robbers have been blessed, as was one of the two on that day.

Above his cross was inscribed: "JESUS OF NAZARETH THE KING OF THE JEWS." To announce the nature of the crime was a good custom. The heathen took their justice seriously. No one could be condemned without being accused, and no one was executed without having been heard. And this, too, was excellent that at an execution a placard was placed upon the gallows or cross that all might know the offense. Christ was charged with being the King of the Jews. Today we still write it above the cross, though now it has become a title of honor, just as his cross and death have come to be esteemed. The Jews meant it as the greatest reproach.

"Now there stood by the cross of Jesus his mother." (John 19:25.)

What agony Mary endured as she watched his suffering none can comprehend. In all history there is no other account of a woman who followed her son when he must suffer so frightfully. She saw him crowned with thorns, spat upon, and hanged. Truly the sword of Simeon must have gone through her heart. A mother can scarcely stand it if her child falls from a bench or bleeds from the ear. Where shall we find a mother who could see such things as Mary? She could not speak but must watch all the tortures and hear all the revilings as they gave him vinegar to drink and diced for his clothing. To be sure, the Holy Spirit gave her comfort, but other mothers would

The Crucifixion

have fainted. And for Christ, to see his mother suffer was one of the greatest parts of his pain, that nothing should be lacking in his suffering.

In the case of the thief we have an example of Christ's forgiveness. This thief reproved his fellow, saying, "Do you not fear God, you who are in the same condemnation?" These were simple words, but

the heart of the thief was greater than heaven and earth. He did not look upon the weakness of Christ. Instead, he saw what cannot be seen, that Christ was a king. Be not ashamed to become a Christian after the manner of this thief, for he was the first saint in the New Testament through the Passion of Christ. For him, Christ prayed upon the cross. We might all be Christians like him. God grant that we may!

Yet this example is not so easy as it seems. He who would come to Christ must feel himself to be a sinner and believe it. Here is the point at which the faith of the thief had an art above any art of which I am capable. When sin and punishment come together, to say that it is right is the art that no cleric possesses. The thief accepted the punishment and bore it willingly, as if he would say: "I deserve it. I will bear it gladly." He who can do that has already conquered, and he who cannot do it is in great danger. The thief did nothing more than to believe and pray. There was no fasting, no pilgrimage. He turned his eyes to the Lord and said, "Lord, remember me when thou comest into thy Kingdom." These are words of faith. He confessed that Christ was King and that he had a Kingdom and asked to be remembered and that was all.

"And Christ prayed, Father, forgive them; for they know not what they do." (Luke 23:34.)

Who can express such love? His heart was so full of the fire of love that no one can comprehend. In pain and shame he acted as though he felt them not and was thinking only of our sin and God's wrath. Is that not love? He burned and writhed beneath the weight, the spear, the blood, the shame, and wounds, and yet he said, "Father, forgive them; for they know not what they do." Here there is a loveliness that only the eyes of the spirit can discern. He was esteemed a robber, a rascal, a reprobate above all reprobates, yet in the heart he was fairer than the sun.

"There was darkness over all the land." (Matt. 27:45.)

The darkness lasted for three hours, from eleven until two o'clock. He cried, "Eli, Eli, lama sabachthani?" It was not merely the suffering but the reproach that hurt. They taunted him: "He trusted in God; let God save him." These were barbed words which smote not only his ears but his heart. He felt what his cry expressed, that he was forsaken by God, as if to say: "God is just. He would not abandon a just man. You must then be his enemy." Reason always comes to this conclusion on the basis of appearance. The Jews argued, "God lets him hang upon the cross, therefore, he must be an accursed heretic." Such words wrung his heart, for we must remember that Christ was a true man. To me also the words would be very bitter if the devil said, "You are mine." I would collapse. The anguish that Christ here experienced drove him to cry out, "My God, my God, why hast thou forsaken me?" Just as a man, when a sword is about to be driven through his neck, lets out in terror a cry of death, so also Christ. In this he was a man as other men. The Passion that Christ suffered from words was even worse than from blows. It is so also with us when the godless reproach us with venomous gibes and threaten us with the wrath of God. They talk as if it were so, and that stings.

The three hours of darkness were frightful. To Christ it seemed that on his account God had blotted out the sun. That is why Christ cried out. The Jews should have been shaken by his death cry, but they were only the more hardened and said: "The living God is his enemy. That is why he turns to the dead Elijah." Such reproaches hurt Christ more than all the pain. He felt it all as a man.

"And one ran and took a sponge and filled it with vinegar, and put it on a reed, and gave him to drink." (Matt. 27:48.)

What mockery! They should have comforted him. The devil emptied all his wrath upon this man. Read all the recitals of dying, and you will not find anything more terrible than this, that one who was forsaken by God and all creatures should be comforted with vinegar.

"And Jesus cried with a loud voice and yielded up the ghost." (Matt. 27:50.)

Even were it an animal, the onlooker would be deeply moved, but when it is an innocent man and when he is the Son of God! If one should properly consider this, one's heart would burst that God's Son, creator of all things, should let out a cry of death. This is above all sense and understanding. We cannot get to the bottom of it our life long.

We should not center our attention, however, upon what Christ suffered but rather upon why he suffered, and the answer is, "for my sake." I am the one who by my sins have deserved that God be my enemy and mock me, even when I cry that the sun should no more shine, the earth no more bear me, and the rocks be rent. When sins are made plain and the conscience is touched, then a man finds out all that Christ suffered here. Then he, too, will say, "Why hast thou forsaken me?" Therefore, everything that Christ suffered is to be referred to our souls, and the more we exalt the Passion the more clearly do we see our own condemnation. Yet, "I will not be afraid for the terror by night, and though the sun should not shine and I be in the shadow of death, I will fear no evil, for thou art with me. Though the earth cry out against me, I will not fear, for I know that Christ has conquered."

"And the veil of the temple was rent in twain from the top to the bottom; and the earth did quake, and the rocks rent; and the graves were opened." (Matt. 27:51.)

The veil of the temple was rent, the darkness on which no one might look became light. While the veil remained, the gospel was hidden and not openly preached, but now with the death of Christ, all that was of the old Adam and the law was dead and done away. Now that I no longer see an angry judge, but that God has given his Son for me, I behold upon the cross the fiery, fatherly love of God.

"The earth quaked." (Matt. 27:51.)

When the veil was rent and God was made known as Father, then the whole earth shook as we see it today, for now the gospel is preached and the earth quakes and the world persecutes us. The rocks are rent. That means the hearts formerly under the law. The Scripture speaks of stony hearts. Through the power of the gospel, when grace is preached, hearts are rent by love.

"And the graves were opened." (Matt. 27:52.)

His death swallowed up death and the very centurion said, "Truly this was the Son of God." He is an amazing king. Other kings are strong in life, he in death. While he lived he was trodden upon, and his enemies took his life. When he was dead the centurion trembled and commenced to be a Christian. The blood of Christ brings to life

The Crucifixion

not only dead bodies but also the souls of prisoners. The disciples had fled, but this centurion began to confess Christ without fear of all the high priests or of what Pilate and the council might say. Who, then, was master here? Was it not the death of Christ that gave the heathen centurion a new spirit? This is the power of the Passion that it makes men bold to confess Christ. We should see from this that through his death he is the Lord of life and death. Whether, then, we live or die, we are in God's hand.

"When even was come, there came a rich man of Arimathea, named Joseph." (Matt. 27:57.)

He had heard that Christ was more powerful in death than in life, and that this heathen had confessed him. This Joseph was a disciple of Jesus but before had been very timid. He was a member

of the Sanhedrin. Mark implies that he had absented himself when judgment was taken against Jesus because he lacked the courage to attend and say that the deed was wrong, but now that Christ was dead, he came and asked for the body. That was a brave act in the teeth of the leaders of church and state. Suppose somebody today should go against the emperor like that? Joseph could do no greater honor to Jesus than to bury him in his own grave. Such high courage sprang from the death of Christ.

Let us now meditate a moment on the Passion of Christ. Some do so falsely in that they merely rail against Judas and the Jews. Some carry crucifixes to protect themselves from water, fire, and sword, and turn the suffering of Christ into an amulet against suffering. Some weep and that is the end of it. The true contemplation is that in which the heart is crushed and the conscience smitten. You must be overwhelmed by the frightful wrath of God who so hated sin that he spared not his only-begotten Son. What can the sinner expect if the beloved Son was so afflicted? It must be an inexpressible and unendurable yearning that causes God's Son himself so to suffer. Ponder this and you will tremble, and the more you ponder, the deeper will you tremble.

Take this to heart and doubt not that you are the one who killed Christ. Your sins certainly did, and when you see the nails driven through his hands, be sure that you are pounding, and when the thorns pierce his brow, know that they are your evil thoughts. Consider that if one thorn pierced Christ you deserve a hundred thousand.

The whole value of the meditation of the suffering of Christ lies in this, that man should come to the knowledge of himself and sink and tremble. If you are so hardened that you do not tremble, then you have reason to tremble. Pray to God that he may soften your heart and make fruitful your meditation upon the suffering of Christ, for we of ourselves are incapable of proper reflection unless God instill it.

But if one does meditate rightly on the suffering of Christ for a day, an hour, or even a quarter of an hour, this we may confidently say is better than a whole year of fasting, days of psalm singing, yes, than even one hundred Masses, because this reflection changes the whole man and makes him new, as once he was in baptism.

If, then, Christ is so firmly planted in your heart, and if you are become an enemy to sin out of love and not fear, then henceforth, the suffering of Christ, which began as a sacrament, may continue lifelong as an example. When tribulation and sickness assail you, think how slight these are compared to the thorns and the nails of Christ. If you are thwarted, remember how he was bound and dragged. If pride besets you, see how the Lord was mocked and with robbers despised. If unchastity incites your flesh, recall how his flesh was scourged, pierced, and smitten. If hate, envy, and vengeance tempt you, think how Christ for you and all his enemies interceded with tears, though he might rather have avenged himself. If you are afflicted and cannot have your way, take heart and say, "Why should I not suffer when my Lord sweat blood for very anguish?"

Astounding it is that the cross of Christ has so fallen into forgetfulness, for is it not forgetfulness of the cross when no one wishes to suffer but rather to enjoy himself and evade the cross? You must personally experience suffering with Christ. He suffered for your sake and should you not suffer for his sake, as well as for your own?

Two texts in the Old Testament apply to Christ. The first is, "Thou art fairer than the children of men" (Ps. 45:2), and the second is, "He hath no form nor comeliness" (Isa. 53:2). Evidently these passages must be understood in differing senses. To the eyes of the flesh, he was the lowest among the sons of men, a derision, and to the eyes of the spirit there was none fairer than he. The eyes of the flesh cannot see this. What, then, is the nature of this beauty? It is wisdom and love, light for the understanding, and power for the soul, for in suffering and dying Christ displayed all the wisdom and truth with which the understanding can be adorned. All the treasures of wisdom and knowledge are hidden in him, and they are hidden because they are visible only to the eye of the spirit.

The greater and the more wonderful is the excellence of his love by contrast with the lowliness of his form, the hate and pain of his Passion. Herein we come to know both God and ourselves. His beauty is his own and through it we learn to know him. His uncomeliness and Passion are ours, and in them we know ourselves, for what he suffered in the flesh, we must inwardly suffer in the spirit. He has in truth borne our stripes. Here, then, in an unspeakably clear mirror you see yourself. You must know that through your sins you are as uncomely and mangled as you see him here.

If we consider the persons, we ought to suffer a thousand and again a thousand times more than Christ because he is God and we are dust and ashes, yet it is the reverse. He, who had a thousand and again a thousand times less need, has taken upon himself a thousand and again a thousand times more than we. No understanding can fathom nor tongue can express, no writing can record, but only the inward feeling can grasp, what is involved in the suffering of Christ.

9

The Resurrection

The Empty Tomb

"Who shall roll away the stone?" (Mark 16:3.)

The angel who sat on the stone and who had driven away the guards was gone. The women were like crazy jackdaws. They thought, "Who will roll away the stone?" They were distressed and supposed they had come for nothing. Still, great love had brought them to the tomb, and they saw that the guards were gone and the stone rolled away. But this did not seem to them to augur any good, for they thought that the Jews had taken away the body to prevent the disciples from doing so. The women entered with heavy hearts, and while they stood, two men appeared before them in shining raiment at whom they dared not look for terror. The angel said, "Why seek ye the living among the dead?"

"He is not here." (Mark 16:6.)

A Christian should be where Christ is. If Christ is not here, a Christian should not be here. That is why no one can find Christ or a Christian in any particular set of rules. He is not here. He has left behind the graveclothes, namely, worldly justice, wisdom, piety, law, and the like. You are not to seek him in these things which are to be found on earth. You won't find him in any Carthusian or in any other monastic cowl. You will not find him in fastings, watchings, vestments. These are all graveclothes. Also, all customs and usages of the fathers and the jurists, the wise and the godly, and whatever else there may be, these are only graveclothes. He is not here. He never puts on graveclothes, nor can a Christian.

But now some jump to the wrong conclusion from this, and the Radicals say, since this is so, that we are above all things and not bound to this or that, then, let us do what we please. That is what the peasants did in their insurrection. They wrecked castles, cloisters, and sacked cellars, and all this they called Christian freedom, but you never make yourselves Christians by demolishing cloisters and

despising the government. A Christian is, indeed, above everything on earth, regardless of his station, whether lord or serf, prince or servant, matron or maid. He is a Christian because he clings to One who died and rose again and is no longer here.

But a Christian has still to live with other people. My body still must have wife, children, house, clothes, and food. God does not intend by the gospel to overturn the civil order. He wants the spirit and the heart to rule, but he has left the hands and the feet as he made them. If I believe on Christ, I am at home in my fatherland, but in the body I am a guest. Then, I must behave like other people, uphold the good of the world, and help to maintain the common peace, and, in addition to that, although I am free, I must nevertheless be a servant to every man. I have hands and feet and tongue, eyes, ears; they all belong together, and with them I must be a servant and so live that I may be helpful to others.

The Radicals should preach this and not mix everything up. They are looking for outward freedom, but Christian freedom does not belong on earth, but rather to a better land. Whether, then, you are husband, wife, son, daughter, lord, or servant, do what falls to you. Believe me, it is very difficult to keep apart these two kingdoms.

The women then returned fearful to the city. They had seen indeed the angel but did not listen to him, for one that is in danger of death can scarcely take hold of the words of life.

The dear apostles heard indeed the words of the women that the grave was open and that an angel had been seen. The first they believed readily enough, but that Christ really was alive appeared to them to be an idle tale. The apostles would say, "We think you are a silly crew." The apostles could not see the living Christ because the dead and buried Christ was so impressed upon their thoughts. In periods of depression, it is always so, and if anyone says the contrary, one takes it for a fairy tale.

Mary told Peter and the disciples, "They have taken away the Lord, and we know not where they have laid him" (John 20:2). Though all the women said this, the disciples did not yet believe, and the women then allowed themselves to be persuaded that it was only a fantasy and that they had been deceived. The words of the angel were thus in vain, but Mary Magdalene kept on saying, "They have taken away my Lord."

Then went Peter and John to the tomb. John, who records this very properly, gives Peter the honor of the first place. The papists infer from this that Peter was above John. Now when these came to the grave, they found their unbelief confirmed that the body of the Lord had been taken away as Magdalene had said. Peter then certainly thought: "Christ surely would not have arranged the graveclothes in this fashion. The Jews must have done it." At the sight of the napkin he was doubly sure. So they went forth in unbelief. Why? Because they did not credit the Scripture and did not realize that it predicts the resurrection. The disciples then returned to the city. This was the second visit to the tomb.

In the Garden

The women conferred with Peter and John, but their doubt was only as to who had taken away the body, whether the Jews or Pilate. There was no thought of the resurrection, not so much as a hairbreadth. While the other women had departed, Mary Magdalene remained in the Garden, for women are more fervent. She stayed by the tomb, went in and out, peered, saw two angels, and finally the Lord himself, whom she did not know. This is something to ponder, that the Lord first appeared to Mary Magdalene, and it is something to consider that he first appeared to a woman. This marvelous preaching of the angel was given to a weaker vessel. It is a great comfort that women are the type of those who hear the gospel. In these women there is a great unconquerable strength out of the Word that stands firm against all the assaults of Satan. Those who accept the gospel are the Magdalenes, that is, the weak. The Word that they hear cuts through death and sin.

Mary spoke to Christ, whom she took to be the gardener, saying, "Sir, if thou have borne him hence, tell me where thou hast laid him, and I will take him away" (John 20:15). The text implies that she had then fallen to the ground at his feet and was about to touch him. Jesus said to her, "Touch me not."

"Touch me not." (John 20:17.)

If you would hear a sermon, listen to this. I cannot fathom it. "Touch me not; for I am not yet ascended to my Father: but go to my brethren, and say unto them, I ascend unto my Father, and your Father; unto my God, and your God." Magdalene was not to touch him because she did not yet believe. She thought that Christ was come again in the life in which he had been before and would so remain. Christ said there was now to be no more touching as among friends. "I do not need ointment any more." With these words Christ said farewell to everything on earth. He had withdrawn from the land of the living, as Isaiah said (Isa. 53:8). A partition had come between him and this world; we are divided.

But Mary was not rejected. He said to her, "Go say unto my brethren." First he said good-by and that he would have nothing more to do with them, and now that he would give them everything. These two sayings are absolutely contradictory. First, he would not be touched, and now he would be a brother. If we are brothers, we should be able not only to touch but to embrace. This is a strange preaching. First he tells Mary to rise and stand off, and now he calls her "dear sister." That was wonderful, and I cannot preach about it as I ought. "Go say unto my brethren." Think of what is being said. Christ is dead, buried, risen from the dead, departed from this life, without brothers and sisters, and will recognize no one. This is clear-cut. It is as if he said, "I have no one on earth," and then he speaks of brethren. There must then be a heavenly and an earthly element here bound together. He who would be a Christian, let him learn these words, "You are my brethren."

What does "brethren" mean? The disciples had all fled. They had no reason to think that they had any claim to be even servants. How overjoyed they must have been when he raised up Mary and said, "Go say unto my brethren"! That word should have raised three hundred thousand from the dead. If only they could believe it! The words are there; one has but to believe. But how? Peter had denied; the others had fallen away. How did they deserve to be called "brethren"? That means to have the same seat and right as Christ, save only that he was the first-born among many brethren, but in the inheritance they were the same. One who is a brother is neither a lord nor a servant. There is no greater word in all Scripture than this one, "Go say unto my brethren."

If the king of France or of England were to say, "You shall be my brother," and he really meant it, one would assume, "He who does anything to me is doing it to the king's brother and where the king sits and eats and rests, there, too, I may be." But no one considers who it is who speaks these words in the Gospel, for in that case, the brother would become such a lord, that no one could comprehend. For what is Christ? The greatest lordliness is in that word "brethren."

If, then, we are his brothers, we are in the same inheritance and rights as he. We are not, indeed, Christ himself, but we enjoy the same privileges, and since he ascends to the Father, then, the Father and Christ and the brethren will be made, as it were, into one loaf. He who can believe that is a Christian.

Journey to Emmaus

There are two difficulties in believing the account of the resurrection. The first is that the work itself is so overpowering that in this life we can never comprehend it even though faith be strong and no weakness be involved. But, as a matter of fact, there is weakness. The first difficulty God cannot mitigate. The work must and should remain as great as it is and nothing be taken from it. This is the power and the might before which all creatures, men, angels, devil, and hell must quail and fail because if this were not so, we should have to remain under our sins and the eternal wrath of God and death. But, as for the second difficulty, that we are too weak to grasp so great a work and power in faith, God is able to look through his fingers and be patient. That is what Christ did with his disciples, who had indeed heard that he was risen, but were in such doubt that they questioned Christ himself, for they said, "We trusted that it had been he who should have redeemed Israel."

See with what care Christ gave himself to these two weak believers, how he did everything to help their weakness and strengthen their faith, because he saw and knew why they were so troubled and why they had withdrawn from the other apostles not knowing what to think or hope. The Lord would not leave them in doubt and torment but went to their aid. That was why he joined them on the way and left all the other apostles by themselves, although they also were troubled and weak enough in the faith. But because these two were in such great danger of unbelief, he suddenly joined them, as if, after his resurrection, he had nothing else whatever to do. He talked and disputed with them in such a friendly way out of the Scriptures and gave them occasion to invite him to lodge with them, to eat and to drink with them until their faith was awakened, their doubt dispelled, and they knew that he was the Christ whom they had known before and had seen crucified only three days ago but could not now recognize while on the way by reason of their doubt and weakness.

As "they drew nigh unto the village, whither they went: he made as though he would have gone further. But they constrained him, saying, Abide with us." (Luke 24:28–29.)

That was the prayer of good folk. God permitted them to invite Christ, though they did not yet know that this was to be their salvation. Such prayer is good, but the means which we propose, God rejects. That is what happens to us; God often comes in other ways and better ways to our help.

"And he went in to tarry with them. . . . And he took bread, and blessed it, and brake, and gave to them." (Luke 24:30.)

The bread is the gospel and consists in this, that Christ must suffer and enter into his glory. What he had just said in words, he now made clear in a figure. He gave them the broken and consecrated bread, that is, Christ in his Passion.

"And their eyes were opened, and they knew him; and he vanished out of their sight." (Luke 24:31.)

Why did he vanish? When the goodness of Christ and God have been revealed and our consciences are comforted, then he goes away and leaves us hanging on the cross. Those two disciples lost his presence, but the knowledge of him they never lost again. His presence was sweet, just as his word is sweet to us, but when he vanishes, the cross takes hold, and we shudder as if he were far, far away. He does not leave his word unassailed, for after the breaking of the bread, he vanishes.

"And they rose up the same hour, and returned to Jerusalem." (Luke 24:33.)

This means that where the gospel is not known, one cannot be silent. It is impossible that it should not be proclaimed to all men.

And being gathered with the disciples he said unto them, "Why are ye troubled? and why do thoughts arise in your hearts?" Then he not only showed the prints on his hands but asked them to give him something to eat. He had no need to do this. It was for the sake of the disciples. Previously he had had need to eat and did not wish to tempt God. He did, therefore, as a man does. So should we also. I am not under the law. My heart is free, but I can do something for the sake of another. If [the Radicals] wear gray cloaks, so also can I, not that I gain any merit by it, but for the sake of my neighbor.

"Then opened he their understanding, that they might understand the Scriptures, And said unto them, Thus it is written, and thus it behooved Christ to suffer, and to rise from the dead the third day: And that repentance and remission of sins should be preached in his name." This means that all men must be told that they are sinners. All have fallen short of the glory of God, and if one says five Pater Nosters and puts on a cowl, and his heart remains unchanged, this is no repentance. The heart must be different. The heart must be good. Repentance must come inwardly.

The article on the resurrection is the most important but the most difficult to believe. The others are hard, but this exceeds them all because no article so contradicts experience as does this, for we see how all men die and how bodies are mutilated. Some are devoured by wild beasts; one man leaves a leg behind in Hungary, another is burned, another drowned, and yet we are to believe that the members will be reassembled and we shall have the same bodies, the same eyes, and so on, although in an altered form. When one reflects on this, it seems as if this article were either nothing at all or, at any rate, quite uncertain. Only a few really believe it. Among the Jews only one half believed either in the resurrection or in angels. The Sadducees did not. When reason considers this article, it simply lets it go. That is why we have to have the Scripture for it.

I have found from experience that the devil can undo me the more easily when I am not armored with the Word. He has brought me to the point where I do not know if there is a God or a Christ, and has taken from me what otherwise I know for certain. That is what happens if the heart is without the Word and faith.

The Power and the Victory

We have heard how the resurrection happened, and now we come to the way in which it is to be received. The resurrection should be impressed upon the whole Christian life. This is the power of faith in works. Those who faint need indeed to be told that Christ has done it all, and there is no need for us to do anything. At the same time no one is under grace who continues in sin. If you are free from sin and not subject to sin, you should not sin. Otherwise, you give proof that you are not free from sin. Justification by faith corresponds to the divine nature of Christ and good works to the human nature. They must become one person, just as in Christ divinity and humanity are conjoined.

[Then again, lest such a passage might lead to any reliance upon good works, Luther would often decry any pretention to perfection. But note how he shifts from actual sin to the sense of sin.] In 1531 he said:

In so far as you believe, you are like Christ, but at the same time feel sin and death. By faith you are one with Christ and with him you are risen from the dead. On the last day it will be manifest, but in the meantime, there is no difference between a Christian and any other man. The Christian lives in sin as does another, except that the Christian commits no gross sins, and when he falls does not stay down. Yet, a hypocrite often seems better than a true Christian. You will have to leave Christianity and sin together. In the Lord's Prayer there is the confession that we need forgiveness.

At the death of Christ the sun was darkened, but at the resurrection there were not many miracles. This may have been lest we lose ourselves in speculating night and day about the miracles and miss in so doing the true use of the resurrection. See now what Christ had done to the apostles when he died. They had supposed he would be king of the world. When, then, he died, they were desolate and felt as if they were dead themselves. Thus, God desired that the suffering of Christ should be at work in his disciples. Similarly through the resurrection the disciples were renewed and lived again. And how did that happen, if not by the resurrection? It must be powerful, inasmuch as there can be only death and affliction in the Passion. Paul says, "We are buried with him by baptism" (Rom. 6:4) and "For thy sake, we are killed all the day long. We are counted as sheep for the slaughter" (Ps. 44:22). Why must we suffer such things? It is in order that we may be made conformable to Christ.

"But thanks be to God, which giveth us the victory through our Lord Jesus Christ." (I Cor. 15:57.) What does that mean? There Paul speaks of a wonderful war. This victory has come to us through Christ, and if we have the victory, we can win the war. The devil had sought to destroy Christ and had incited the Jews. They contrived by craft to take the Lord. He had done many miracles, but on the cross he was weak. Others he had helped, himself he could not help. He became a sham and they mocked his words, saying, "He has made himself to be the Son of God." Then the people turned away from him. He had predicted that he would come again. For that reason the grave was securely guarded and his enemies supposed that Christ was entirely destroyed, but then arose the goodness of God and confounded the wiles of the devil, for the Divine Majesty could not connive with all this. God summoned the devil. "Satan," said he, "you have done all the ill you could to me, but I am still alive." This is the miracle which God showed in the person of Christ.

He was eternal life. Blessing and righteousness now fought against curse and death. Temporal death is now nothing against eternal life. It is as if you should try to contain the sea in a little vessel. Paul said not that Christ had overcome sin but that he had swallowed up sin. (I Cor. 15:55.) Hosea said, "Death, I will be thy death." (Hos. 13:14.) This is a fine word, to be the death of death. This victory is given through the gospel, as Paul said. (I Cor. 15:57.) If only I believe that Christ won this victory not for himself but that we may be saved and may be lords of all creatures, not for our sakes, but for the Lord!

Just as Christ won the victory only through struggle, so also must we. If his resurrection is to work in us, we too cannot escape the struggle with death. God has permitted the old man to be at hand. The resurrection lays hold and says that whatever is of us is nothing, and I believe that when the resurrection begins to work in me, then sin and the bad conscience are dead with Christ. But from this follows that the body must die. I feel sin and death in me. The body delights in sin and fears death, and this war we must carry on so long as we live. The Lord assails us with many sufferings. This is the fight, and we must say, "Death, I will be thy death." Death assaults me, but I have Christ who is risen from the dead, as I also shall rise. I will hold to this. The resurrection consists not in words, but in life and power. The heart should take inward delight in this and be joyful. Outwardly, I must die as Christ died, but the gospel is a jubilant word, which the flesh hears gladly. Yet, it has no effect unless we feel it both inwardly, as well as outwardly.

Feed My Sheep

After his resurrection, Jesus appeared to his disciples and said to them, "Feed my sheep." In the Roman Church, "feed" is taken to mean the burdening of Christendom with many heavy, human laws, the selling of bishops' mantles at the highest price, the hauling in of annates from all benefices, the reservation of all foundations, the subjugation of bishops by abominable oaths, the selling of indulgences, the forbidding of the preaching of the gospel, the plaguing of the whole world with briefs, bulls, and seals of lead and wax, the filling of sees all over the world with Romanists, and, in a word, preventing anyone from coming to the truth and living in peace.

Nobody can feed Christ's sheep unless he has love. Now tell me, if you can, whether the papacy displays such love. I am reproached as biting and vindictive, but I am troubled lest I have done too little. I ought to have taken the ravening wolves by the jaws because they constantly rend, poison, and twist the Scriptures to the corruption of the poor, miserable sheep of Christ. If I had enough love, I would have done otherwise to the pope and the Romanists who, with their laws, indulgences, and other tomfoolery, make the Word of God and faith to be of no avail.

It was to Peter that Christ said, "Feed my sheep." If this command had been given to Peter exclusively, which it was not, we should not suppose that only Peter was to feed sheep, and Paul and the other apostles were to feed mice and lice. And if it were given only to Peter, we could not assume that the pope, like Peter, should be the only one to feed *all* the sheep. The Roman congregation had the gospel for a full twenty-five years before Peter or Paul arrived in Rome, and a church is a true church no matter whether it was founded by an apostle or only by a disciple. Antioch and Alexandria were important churches alongside of Rome, and at Antioch, the disciples were first called Christians. If that had happened in Rome, the ten astronomical heavens would not be great enough to contain Roman pride. But, all churches are alike. The pope says, "I am of Peter," whereas Paul forbade these party cries. Suppose the Emperor Charles had a governor in Brabant, and this governor started out to rule also in Spain, Italy, and Germany where the emperor had appointed other governors, would that not be overstepping? I am a preacher at Wittenberg and responsible for the sheep here but not for the sheep in all the other parishes, which have their own preachers.

Moreover, the shepherd should feed the sheep without reward other than the reward of the prophets who were stoned, and that is what has happened to us at the hands of the papists. In these last twenty years many have been strangled, imprisoned, and executed with fire, water, and the sword, or driven out from land and house, from wife and child, and all on account of our feeding the sheep.

As the sun makes the day, so also does the radiance from Christ stream into all believing hearts and is at the same time in them all. As many eyes can see perfectly the rays of the sun, though there is only one sun, and as everyone has this ray perfectly, and all of them have it together, so is it also with Christ. We have him altogether and yet each has him in his own heart. When he comes he lightens and rules us all through one faith. Then falsehood disappears and the heart rightly sees God's Word and work. There is then a new world, a new people, and a new light.

Sources

The references are to the Weimar edition of Luther's works. The citation 17,i,17.12–20.38 means volume 17, part one (which is a separate volume), page 17, line 12 to page 20, line 38. "Excerpted" means that out of a section of numerous pages paragraphs have been excerpted. "Condensed" means that in one or more paragraphs sentences or phrases have been selected and blended.

Chapter 1
The Coming of The Redeemer
   The Prologue
      10,i,183.1–12
      10,i,198.16–22
      10,i,209.18–210.4
      27,531–533
      27,533.8–534.4
      29,32
      37,8.36–9.2
      46,712.6–16
   The Genealogies
      53,610–611
   The Annunciation
      7,549
      12,458.35–459.12
      9,627.20
      17.1.150.23–152
   The Visitation
      41.352.23–353.9
      46,475
      41,353.19

      27,231 41,353–356
      36,210.13–24
      41,358.27–359.7
   The Magnificat
      41,360.2–11
      41,361.22–363.16
      7,559.31 f.
      41,363–365
      7,566.19–567.20
      7,575.4–23
      7,581.35–583.28 7,587
      12.609.1–9
      7,590.3–9. cf.29,457–458
      7,593.25–594.7
      7.596.1–7
      600,33–35
   The Boyhood of Jesus
      TR 5,89–91. no.5360
   The Boy Jesus Lost in the Temple
      17,ii,17.12–20.38

Chapter 2

Beginnings of the Ministry
  The Feast of Epiphany and the Baptism
    34,i,21–31 and 42–50
  The Temptations
    17,ii,196.15–30 and
    37,308.20–25
    17,0,187.18–189 17,i,64.3
    5–65.4
    17.11.193.1–194.13
    46,206.18–24 17,ii,195
    54.264.33–265.13
  The Call of the First Disciples: Of Peter and Andrew, who Left Their Nets, and James and John, who Left Their Boat and Their Father
    1,101.8–102.12
    The Marriage at Cana
    17,ii,65.24–67.34
    17,i,29–32
    17,ii,63–64
    17.ii.62.1–5 27,24.26–25.16
    36,91 and 17,ii,62.17–27
    36,92.5–96.6
  Nicodemus
    12.588.25–591.8
    15,568; 20,416.11; 423.7–27
    20.426.33–429.5
    41,610.39–611.18
  The Woman at the Well
    47.220.12–29; 226.40–227.5
  The Woman Who Was a Sinner, Who Washed the Master's Feet
    41.647.25–648.10
  The Beheading of John the Baptist
    37.462.13–464.20

    8,581.19 f. 45,112.8–13
    20.456.2–10
    11.252.12–24
  The Beatitudes
    9,416–419
    34,i,85.21–23
  The Parables of Salt and Light
    32,343–345
    32.351.38–352.5
    32,352.33–353.6
  The Law
    39.i.571.10–574.5
    11,149.22–31
    11.148.3–13
    1.494.38–496.22
    1,435.11–23
    6,40.9–29
  Almsgiving
    32,409.32–410.6
  The Lord's Prayer
    30,i,197.2–5
    30,i,198–199
    2,98.34–40
    2,104.31–105.16
    30,i,204.1–205.19
  "When Ye Fast"
    32.429.13–432.16, condensed
  "Lay Not Up for Yourselves Treasures Upon Earth"
    32.439.20–441
  On Anxiety
    1,82.18–83.22
    27.346.10–347.27
  "Judge Not"
    29,405.5–406
    36.191.21–26
  The Narrow Gate
    32,500.12–503

Chapter 3
The Sermon on The Mount
  The Ethic

Chapter 4
The Miracles and the Parables
  The Cure of the Deaf and Dumb

Sources

46.493.19–494.22
  The Widow's Son 11,181.13 F.
    15.680.25–28
    32.123.11–124.14
    11,182.22–27
  The Miracle of the Loaves and Fishes
    27.274.11–276.9; 277.2–8; 279.1–280.7
    29.468.25–26
    34,ii,19.12–14
    15.651.20–652.20
    36,125.7–21
    17,i,155.23–156.7
  The Cure of the Nobleman's Son
    10.iii.424.32–425.22
    34,ii,355.9–13; 357,12–13
  Peter's Failure to Walk on the Water
    38.580.32–581.9
  The Canaanite Woman
    17,ii,202.38 f.
  The Parable of the Sower
    17,ii,157.33–154.23, condensed
  The Parable of the Tares
    17,ii,124.6–125.16
    52,825.1–21
    51,174.16–175.23, condensed
    51,181,29–183.9, condensed
  The Good Samaritan
    56,272.3–21; 2,586.14–19
  The Great Banquet
    41,286.19–32; 287.14; 288.27; 289.18–200.2
  The Lost Sheep
    15,633.5–634.9;
    36,294.4–295.5; 300.5–7
  The Prodigal Son
    2,362.23–25; 43,175.20–26
  The Rich Man and Lazarus
    10,iii, 178.19–187.29, excerpted
  The Grateful Samaritan
    8,378.25–379.20
  The Pharisee and the Publican
    10.iii.296.13–17; 301.2–17

Chapter 5
The Journey to Jerusalem and Holy Week
  Fire from Heaven
    45,409.1–31
  Peter's Confession
    2,189.28–190.40
  Peter and the Keys
    30.ii.455.13–26
  Peter and Tax Collecting
    38,666.10–32
  "Except Ye Become as Little Children"
    37,156.18–24; 158.13–18; 159.22–160.23
  "Who is my Mother? And Who Are my Bretheren?"
    28,25.3–18
  "Come Unto Me"
    23,690.34–691.35
  "Where Two or Three Are Gathered Together"
    47,298.4–21
  Zaccheaus 1,97.29–40
  Jerusalem Beleaugured
    34,ii,88.9–92.1
  Mary and Martha
    10,iii,269.22–270.21
  Palm Sunday
    10,i,2,22.21–23.8; 30.22–26; 37.32–38.25; 39.12–14
  The Cleansing of the Temple
    46,726.31–736.33, condensed
  "Let Not Your Heart Be Troubled"
    45,468.13–463.19; 470.31–471.17

"Ye Believe in God, Believe also in Me"
  11,111.23–112.1
Temples of God
  15.565.2–11
"God so Loved the World"
  36,180.21–182.7
  37,410.18–24; 410.29–412.16
"My peace I Give Unto You"
  11.114.2–8
"When the Comforter Comes"
  10,iii, 150.7–26
All Shall Bear Witness
  29,341.8–19
Asking the Father
  28,56.25–57.10
"I Know My Sheep"
  37,73.1–11

Chapter 6
The Lord's Supper
  An Outward Sign
    [1520] 6,538.35–539.5
  Not An Untouchable Charm
    [1522] 10,iii,70.28–71.22
  Inward and Unconstrained
    [1522] 10,iii,48.7–54.12
  Also Outward
    [1525] 18,164.31–165.3;
    166.29–34; 168.15–170.25;
    180.17–20
  Christ's Body Not in Heaven
    [1527] 23,131.7–15;
    135.35–37; 139.12–140.10;
    145.13–32; 150.25–32
  Do Not Mess or Pry into the Inscrutable
    [1534] 37,348.16–349.19
    [1519] 2,749.23–750.13
  Let the Unexamined Abstain
    [1523] 12,477.20
  But the Timorous are Invited

  [1528] 30,i,227.5–25;
  229,10–15
  [1529] 29,209.1–210.16
  [1534] 37,349.19–350.10
The Sacrament of Love
  [1522] 10,iii,55.3–58.5
Fellowship
  [1519] 2,743,7–35; 745.45–46
  [1528] 30,i,26.31–37
  [1519] 2,748.6–26

Chapter 7
Arrest and Trail
  On What to Meditate
    41,41.10–42.18
    17,i,352.21–353.7
  Anointing in Bethany
    46.242.19–246.10,
    condensed
  Washing of the Disciples' Feet
    29. 223.8–10
    46.277.9–18
    29,223.16–224.5
    46.287.1–7
    46.295.19–297.2
    20,310.28–311.2
  Gethsemane
    28,205.37–209.5
    28,210.6–214.3
    28,245.10–252.10
  Trial before Annas and Peter's Denial
    28,258.5–261.7
    28,268.8–273.4
    28.279.2–289.8
  Trial Before Pilate
    28,298–393, excerpted

Chapter 8
The Crucifixion
  28.385.10–393
  34,1,250

29,244.16–247.12
37,355.21–32
17,1,67–84, excerpted
2,136–141
1,337.10–344.10, excerpted

Chapter 9
The Resurrection
  The Empty Tomb
    29,258.19–259.24
    32,49.29–52.2, excerpted
    29,259.7–277.9, excerpted
  In The Garden
    27,116.5–10
    29,294.9–297.4, excerpted
    29.292.2–301.5, excerpted
  Journey to Emmaus
    21,255.17–226.19
    15,528.29–529.24
    20,349.11–350.18

28.429.22–431.14
32,58.18–22
The Power and the Victory
  27,124.31–125.8
  34,i,275.13–276.3
  15.517.23–519.20
Feed My Sheep
  6,306.20–34
  6,319.12–320.21–33
  54.275.3–278.8
  9,669.10–18

You may also be interested in:

Transfiguring Luther

The Planetary Promise of Luther's Theology

by Vítor Westhelle

Luther's theology has inspired many since 1517 when he nailed his ninety-five theses to the door of the Castle Church. It was the trigger of the Reformation, a change in the very fabric of Christianity that is still studied extensively to this day. Much of this work however has been conducted from either a European or North American perspective. With Lutheranism becoming more and more common in the southern hemisphere, new interpretations of Luther's theology are needed for these emergent and different contexts.

In *Transfiguring Luther*, Vítor Westhelle offers a reading of Luther and his legacy that goes beyond the traditional geopolitics of Luther research, exploring realities where the Reformer's reception and the latent promise of his theology receive unsuspected appraisal. Westhelle provides both a revisitation of the past and an invitation to a new orientation. By establishing a texture rather than a rigid actuality, Westhelle allows the reader to reach their own conclusions about these seldom examined aspects of Luther's theology.

> 'of great importance for anyone wanting to understand world Lutheranism...'
> – **David Carter,** in *The Window,* 2017

Vítor Westhelle is Professor of Systematic theology at the Lutheran School of Theology at Chicago and the chair of Luther Research at Faculdades EST, São Leopoldo, Brazil. A well-known author and internationally sought-out speaker.

Published 2017

Paperback ISBN: 978 0 227 17650 4
PDF ISBN: 978 0 227 90631 6

You may also be interested in:

Luther's Revolution

The Political Dimensions of Martin Luther's Universal Priesthood

by Nathan Montover

In this eloquent and informative work, Nathan Montover challenges the widespread assumption that Martin Luther was a conservative and politically naive figure. Montover uses the prism of Luther's doctrine of Universal Priesthood to reveal a politically aware individual determined not only to reform the Christian ministry, but also to radically challenge the temporal power structures of his day.

An excellent addition to Lutheran scholarship, this book is suitable for any reader interested in Luther's life and aims or the fascinating political ferment of the Reformation.

> *'Luther emerges from this excellent study as a throughly political, prophetic, and revolutionary Christian engaged in the struggle for liberation, drawing radical political consequences from foundational theological claims.*
> – **Craig L. Nessan,** Professor of Contextual Theology, Wartburg Theological Seminary

Nathan Montover serves as pastor at St James Lutheran Church in Iowa. He also teaches Religion at Augustana College in Illinois, and is Asjunct Instructor of Reformation Studies at Wartburg Theological Seminary in Iowa.

Published 2012

Paperback ISBN: 978 0 227 68014 8
PDF ISBN: 978 0 227 90116 8